W9-BSO-062

WITHDRAWN

Form and Convention
in the Poetry of
Edmund Spenser

FORM AND CONVENTION

IN THE POETRY OF

EDMUND SPENSER

Selected Papers from the English Institute

Edited with a Foreword by WILLIAM NELSON

New York and London

Columbia University Press

Foreword

ALTHOUGH THE ESSAYS in this collection differ widely in subject and in approach there lies behind them a common assumption which an editorial preface should make explicit. Whether or not the contributors represent the current trend of opinion about Spenser, they appear to be agreed that his poems are complex and subtly constructed units and that the chief task of the scholar or critic is to lay bare the principles of their structure. This direction of effort contrasts sharply with the tendency of those writers who emphasize the structural defects and inconsistencies of thought, mood, and style in his poetry. The division I have drawn is no doubt too sharp, for few of Spenser's commentators would identify themselves without reservation as of one or the other camp, but its general validity is documented by the history of Spenser criticism from its very beginnings.

In his *Discourse concerning the Original and Progress of Satire* John Dryden, generally an enthusiastic admirer of *The Faerie Queene,* reserved his severest censure for the inadequacy of its plan: "For there is no uniformity in the design of Spenser:

he aims at the accomplishment of no one action. . . . Had he lived to finish his poem, in the six remaining legends, it had certainly been more of a piece; but could not have been perfect, because the model was not true." Thomas Warton quite agreed: "Spenser, and the same may be said of Ariosto, did not live in an age of planning. His poetry is the careless exuberance of a warm imagination and a strong sensibility. It was his business to engage the fancy, and to interest the attention by bold and striking images, in the formation, and the disposition of which, little labour or art was applied." But Warton's contemporary John Upton took a position directly contrary: "In every poem there ought to be simplicity and unity; and in the epic poem the unity of the action should never be violated by introducing any ill-joined or heterogeneous parts. This essential rule Spenser seems to me strictly to have followed." The dispute is by no means confined to *The Faerie Queene*. The first editor of *The Shepheardes Calender,* Spenser's friend "E.K.," described its principal merit as the tightness of its construction: "For what in most English wryters useth to be loose, and as it were ungyrt, in this Authour is well grounded, finely framed, and strongly trussed up together." Yet in his edition of the same poem Professor W. L. Renwick finds it necessary to suppose that the scheme of the *Calender* is a superficial afterthought: "We may imagine that some time in 1579 Spenser at last decided to publish some of his accumulated poems; he had some pastorals by him, and it was in accordance with critical theory that he should begin with them; the idea of the Calendar came to him because they contained definite seasonal references after the manner of Mantuan, and perhaps because he had about twelve, and could easily make up, or cut down, to that number." One student of the *Amoretti* understands it to be a single poem in which each quatorzain is a stanza; another concludes that it is an unsuccessful blending of two very different collections of sonnets. Some of Spenser's critics have high praise for his harmonious union of style and matter; others detect a schizoid disjunct between the kind of poetry Spenser was born to write and the kind of poetry he thought it his duty to write.

I have, to be sure, oversimplified the controversy. There are those who find unity in one poem and not in another, and those who think that Spenser indeed planned but could not execute. The most ardent defenders of the unity and coherence of the poems must admit that there are discrepancies between the narrative of *The Faerie Queene* and its description in the letter to Ralegh, and they are unable to account in terms of literary structure for the disappearance of Amoret at a critical moment in the Legend of Friendship, the author's uncertainty as to whether Britomart's traveling companion is the Red Cross Knight or Sir Guyon, and his assignment of a poem apparently written for February to November in *The Shepheardes Calender*. For these and similar slips they offer the explanation that such matters represent merely the debris of Spenser's architectural effort and should not distract the critic from the essential building. Those of the opposite party grant, necessarily, that since the poems are the work of a strongly individual poetic talent—that is, since no one else could have written them—they have a unity of kind. They argue, nevertheless, that there is a difference between the young and the mature Spenser and that many of the poems, written early and later revised, are the confused product of a confusion of the two.

The way in which the difference in critical bias affects the reading of Spenser's poems may be shown by a single minor instance. Sonnet 83 of the *Amoretti* is a repetition of Sonnet 35. This circumstance leads Professor Renwick to the hypothesis that Spenser rearranged the sonnet series before publication and in the process destroyed "its integrity, if it had any." The same circumstance suggests to Professor Martz the possibility that the repetition was deliberately calculated for its effect upon the reader of the sequence as a whole. The hypotheses are offered tentatively by both critics; they betray, nevertheless, the significant divergence of their views and the pervasive effect of such divergences.

The judgment of disunity in Spenser's poems is often linked with speculation as to the history of their composition. Although the connection is not inevitable it seems natural enough, for a work which is at odds with itself invites inquiry as to why it is so. Miss Spens has argued that *The Faerie Queene* was originally planned as eight books of eight cantos each, Mrs. Bennett that it began as a continuation of Chaucer's tale of Sir Thopas, and other scholars have proposed other beginnings. Similar efforts have been devoted to *The Shepheardes Calender,* the *Amoretti, The Ruines of Time, Mother Hubberds Tale,* and the *Fowre Hymnes.* These investigations may be immensely valuable as essays towards the poet's biography and the genetic history of his work, but they can tell us little of the nature of that work. A seed determines the kind of tree which grows from it; the relationship of a fully developed concept and the germ from which it sprang, however, remains mysterious. Nor is there any necessary connection between the structural quality of a literary product and the vicissitudes of its gestation, for incoherence is as easy to achieve extempore as with long labor. There is no reason to doubt that Spenser authorized the publication of his poems (with the exception of the posthumously printed cantos of "Mutability," to be sure) and we must suppose that he considered them finished works, or in the case of *The Faerie Queene* finished parts. The poems themselves, and not their histories, must determine whether they are artistic units, careless patchworks of miscellaneous materials, or the products of a disorganized or divided mind.

The duration of this dispute is evidence that it cannot easily be resolved. On the one hand, that which is proposed as the essential structure of a poem may be merely the fiction of its discoverer, as the configurations of the sky are the invention of the star-gazer. On the other hand, failure to perceive form may demonstrate not formlessness but a defect in the observer. In the richly various forest of Spenser's poems it is easy both to imagine paths that do not exist and to deny the reality of those that do.

The contributors to this book are agreed that the paths are there, but the charts they provide are by no means identical. Professor Smith emphasizes Spenser's use of established literary conventions to provide his readers with frames of reference, Professor Martz considers the *Amoretti* in terms of the complexity and consistency of its tone, Professor Hieatt believes that he has uncovered a recondite arrangement of stanzas in the *Epithalamion* which subserves its intention, Professor Hamilton tries to define the allegorical method of *The Faerie Queene* by reference to the method of *Piers Plowman,* Professor Berger follows the thread of Spenser's meditations on the relationship between the poet and the world he imitates, and Dr. Hawkins argues for the thematic integrity of the "Cantos of Mutabilitie." Nevertheless, these approaches are not mutually exclusive, and in fact they tend in the same direction. Whether the principal concern of the essayists is with form, tone, method, or theme, their goal appears to be to demonstrate by means of historical research and careful study of the poems that Spenser was a highly sophisticated, self-conscious, and meticulous artist.

With the exception of those by Professors Hamilton and Berger, the papers in this collection were delivered before the meetings of the English Institute in 1959 and 1960. The paper presented by Mr. Hamilton at the 1959 meeting is now a chapter of his book, *The Structure of Allegory in The Faerie Queene* (Oxford, 1961). That which here appears under his name develops the ideas of an article he originally published in *Studies in Philology,* LV (No. 4, 1958), pp. 533–48. Mr. Berger's Institute paper of 1959 has also appeared in print, in *Studies in English Literature,* I (January, 1961), 93–120. In its place he offers the essay included in this volume.

WILLIAM NELSON

Columbia University
New York
March, 1961

Contents

A . C . H A M I L T O N

The Visions of *Piers Plowman* and
The Faerie Queene

MY PURPOSE IN RELATING *The Faerie Queene* to *Piers Plowman* is to see whether they may prove to be mutually illuminating. I know that enormous difficulties may frustrate this purpose: simply each poem's comprehensiveness and complexity. There is less difficulty for readers of Spenser's poem who may be guided by well-established historical and critical backgrounds, though they may lose themselves there as in a Wandering Wood where "so many pathes, so many turnings seene, / That which of them to take, in diuerse doubt they been." Certainly the difficulty is greater for Langland's readers, who need to know so much more about the poem's background—for example, the poet's use of learning—before adequate critical awareness becomes possible. For this reason, modern Langland criticism is historical: it focuses, and quite rightly, upon the poem's content. Yet it should be critical, too, and focus upon the poem's form. However complicated the historical traditions behind the poem, their complexity may be seen only in the poem's control over content through its structure. I believe that its structure may be clarified by comparing it to *The Faerie Queene,* which is the one great architectonic poem to which it is significantly related.[1] While there may be a historical tradition to which the form of *Piers Plowman* is related more directly, if Langland is like the other major poets who emerge so clearly out of their historical context, his poem makes an imaginative leap which brings it into the central tradition of English poetry.

My argument in this paper proceeds in four stages. I need first to offer my reasons for relating Spenser to Langland. Usually Langland is set apart from the central tradition of English poetry which is seen to derive from Chaucer and continue through Spenser to Milton. But Spenser derives from both poets, and his significant affinities in Book I are clearly with Langland. As Milton was the "son" of Spenser, whom he called his "original," Spenser was Langland's son, and within the English tradition Langland was his original. If *Piers Plowman* is ever to be placed in this tradition where it belongs, and the poet regarded as our Homer, the way of doing so will be through *The Faerie Queene*. Secondly, I shall show in detail how Spenser derives from Langland by relating the structure of Book I to the structure of *Piers Plowman*. Thirdly, I shall illustrate one chief difference between the two poems, so that in the final stage of this paper I may compare them as allegories.

I

In the Epilogue to *The Shepheardes Calender* England's "new Poete" places himself in the tradition of Tityrus and "the Pilgrim that the Ploughman playde a whyle," that is, Chaucer and Langland. Spenser refers to those climactic stages in Langland's poem where the pilgrim plays the role of the plowman. There is the crisis of the *Visio* when the field of folk cry upward to Christ for grace to seek Truth, and Piers vows to "ben his [Truth's] pilgryme atte plow for pore mennes sake" (vi.103).[2] When Truth does grant them the pardon they seek, "to peres he sent, / To taken his teme and tulyen the erthe" (vii.1–2). Piers' quarrel with the priest after which he vows to cease ploughing launches the Dreamer into his search for Dowel, Dobet, and Dobest. Piers disappears, except for the inner vision of him guarding the Tree of Charity, until the climax of the *Vita de Dobet,* when he appears once again as the plowman Christ harrowing hell. In the *Vita de Dobest* the Holy Ghost appoints Piers as "my plowman . . . to tulye treuthe" (xix.255–56), that is, to harrow the world for the Apocalypse. The dramatic structure of *Piers Plowman* could hardly be rendered more succinctly than by Spenser's reference. It suggests his close knowledge of the poem.

The relation to Langland which Spenser acknowledges in his Epilogue is shown in the poem. For example, his archaisms evoke Landland's idiom, and his use of the alliterative meter in the *May* eclogue suggests both his meter and matter:

> Some gan to gape for greedie gouernaunce,
> And match them selfe with mighty potentates,
> Louers of Lordship and troublers of states:
> Tho gan shepheards swaines to looke a loft,
> And leaue to liue hard, and learne to ligge soft.

> (121–25)

But more important, the argument of Spenser's poem is the rejection of worldly contentment for the truly dedicated life in this world which Piers alone embodies.[3] Piers plays the same role in Langland's poem. The *Visio* ends when Piers vows to "nought be to bisy aboute the worldes blisse" (vii.125), and the *Vitae* show the Dreamer seeking the three lives which are fulfilled in him. Accordingly there is close affinity between their satire upon the corrupt Church with its worldly prelates. Langland's bitter denunciation of the Church Militant gathers in the cry:

> I shal tellen it for treuth sake take hede who so lyketh!
> As holynesse and honeste oute of holicherche spredeth
> Thorw lele libbyng men that goddes lawe techen,
> Right so out of holicherche alle yueles spredeth,
> There inparfyt presthod is prechoures and techeres.
>
> (xv.89–93)

Similarly, in Spenser's moral eclogues, Piers attacks shepherds who care only for "worldly souenance" (May, l. 82), Thomalin declares "to Kerke the narre, from God more farre" (July, l. 97), and Diggon Davie vows "playnely to speake" against corrupt pastors for "badde is the best" (September, ll. 104–5).

It was inevitable that Spenser would place himself in the tradition of Langland. During his apprenticeship to poetry when decorum demands that he follow earlier poets, the Piers tradition of satire was the only continuous poetic tradition in England which he could imitate. Even to Milton Langland remained the model for English satirists. While he was not limited to the English tradition, that he was led to it is suggested by the title of his critical treatise on "The English Poet." Fortunately the B text of *Piers Plowman* was available for him to read in Crowley's 1550 editions and Owen Rogers' edition of 1561. In reading the poem he lacked that modern historical perspective which reduces it to an expression of orthodox beliefs. For his age it was a covert allegory: "the sence [is] somewhat darcke," Crowley writes, "but not so harde, but that it may be vnderstande of suche as will not sticke to breake the shelle of the nutte for the kernelles sake." [4] It was interpreted as a bitter satire against the Church of Rome and its author honored as a Protestant and a prophet. The poet who declares that "pryde shal be pope prynce of holycherche" (xix.218), who urges that since possessions corrupt the Church "good were to dischargen hem for holicherche sake, / And purgen hem of poysoun or more perile falle" (xv.528–29), and who prophesied the dissolution of the monasteries (an event which may be mirrored in the Kirkrapine episode of *The Faerie Queene*) would appeal strongly to the militantly Protestant Spenser.

Yet he would read Langland's poem as more than a Reformation tract. Piers' break with the Church which precipitates the Dreamer's pilgrimage to seek salvation and brings that firm insistence upon imitating Christ reveals a religious vision central to his own. The Dreamer becomes a radical protestant from that moment when his search for the three lives is initiated through his meeting with the Friars. They counsel him that Dowel dwells among them, for though man commits sins of frailty he may be preserved from deadly sin through exercising his wit and free will. But their counsel is evil, for they allow man to be content with the sins of frailty. Nothing less than total reformation satisfies the Dreamer. Though he is Will himself, he preserves himself only by yielding his will to the other faculties, and in the end by yielding himself to become the servant of the Samaritan-

Christ and entering Unitas. Langland seems closest to Spenser in his simultaneous awareness of the depths of man's depravity and of his potential divinity. But perhaps most important to Spenser, Langland's poem was the unique Christian poem of epic proportions and the single "continued Allegory, or darke conceit" written in England before his time.

II

Spenser's relation to Langland is revealed most clearly in Book I. While he imitates "the antique Poets historicall" in Book II, draws upon romance in Books III and IV, and is manifestly the Renaissance courtly poet in Books V and VI, his first book in its larger outline is centrally Christian, even Catholic and medieval. *Piers Plowman* is related to Book I as analogue rather than source: their concordance reveals the same Christian vision drawn from Scripture and presented in a common language of allegory.

The two poems may be seen to correspond in their larger outlines. Holicherche's instructions to the Dreamer in the prologue is a prelude to the three sections that follow: (1) a vision of Mede corrupting the field of folk until (2) they repent and seek redemption through Christ's death, whereupon (3) Piers gathers them into the body of the Church and ploughs the world in readiness for the Apocalypse. What follows in the three *Vitae* translates what has come before into an inner pilgrimage, and the poem falls into two parallel parts.[5] The Dreamer's wandering which ends with a vision of his sinful state is a prelude to the three sections that follow: (1) a vision of the fallen world of Mede seen in the learned Doctor and Haukyn the *Actiua Vita*,

(2) the *Vita de Dobet* which shows Christ's descent into Hell to redeem mankind, whereupon (3) Piers enters to gather all into Unitas and plough the world in readiness for the coming of Antichrist which heralds the Apocalypse. Similarly, Spenser's book falls into two parallel parts, each with three sections. As the Red Cross Knight's meeting with Error is a prelude to his quest, his meeting with Despair is prelude to his spiritual pilgrimage. 1. Earlier, being guided by Duessa, he enters "a broad high way" leading to the house of Pride; later, guided by Una, he is led on the narrow way to the house of Penance. 2. He leaves the house of Pride only to fall victim to Duessa in league with Orgoglio and the Dragon: he leaves the house of Penance to slay the Dragon and release Una's parents from prison. 3. Earlier, Arthur restores him to Una as a "pined corse" overcome by guilt of sin; finally he becomes fully regenerate and marries Una in triumph. Further, the correspondence between the states marked by the *Vitae* and the three stages of the Knight's spiritual pilgrimage may be indicated by the well-known stages of the mystic way: purgative, illuminative, and unitive.[6] The purgative stage is seen in the *Vita de Dowel,* which shows the sins of the learned Doctor and the repentant Haukyn; the illuminative stage in the *Vita de Dobet,* which shows the exercise of Charity in Christ harrowing Hell to redeem mankind; and the unitive stage in the *Vita de Dobest,* where mankind gathers into Unitas under Piers. Similarly, the Red Cross Knight is purged of his sins in the house of Penance; he exercises the highest degree of charity in slaying the Dragon to release mankind from prison; and finally he marries Una. But the relation between the structure of the two poems is more complex than this rough analogy indicates.

Passus I–V : *Cantos I–V*

Both poems open with the protagonist guided by a lovely lady. Holicherche, "a loueli ladi of lere in lynnen yclothed," instructs the Dreamer not to wander "abouten the mase" of the wilderness but to seek the way to Truth. Una, "a louely Ladie" of radiant whiteness, instructs the Red Cross Knight to "add faith vnto [his] force" in order to overcome Error and leave the Wandering Wood. Crowley terms Langland's prologue "an argument to the whole boke": similarly, Spenser's opening episode is an argument to his book, for it shows the Knight's full power over the woman-serpent while he is guided by Una.

This prelude to the action is followed in both poems by the appearance of evil: Mede corrupts human society, Duessa with Archimago abuses the knight. Mede is "purfiled with pelure . . . hire robe was ful riche of red scarlet engreyned, / With ribanes of red golde and of riche stones" as Duessa is "clad in scarlot red, / Purfled with gold and pearle of rich assay." Holicherche complains that Mede "hath noyed me ful oft, / And ylakked my lemman" (II.20–21) as Una complains that Duessa is "mine onely foe, mine onely deadly dread, / Who . . . inueigled him [the Red Cross Knight] to follow her desires vnmeete" (I.vii.50). The triumph of Mede and Duessa brings a vision of the fallen world anatomized into the seven deadly sins. Langland displays the sins in human form while Spenser presents them in the allegorical pageant in the house of Pride and in Orgoglio. Mede's dominion would be sealed by her marriage to Falsehood which would grant her "the Erldome of enuye and Wratthe togideres . . . the counte of coueitise . . . and al the lordeship of lecherye" until "the route that ran aboute mede" has "a dwellying with the deuel and dampned be for eure . . . and with him to wonye with wo" (II.61, 83–106). Similarly, "the endlesse routs of wretched thralles" who gather in the house of Pride under the rule of Lucifera and Duessa

> mortgaging their liues to *Couetise,*
> Through wastfull Pride, and wanton Riotise,
> They were by law of that proud Tyrannesse
> Prouokt with *Wrath,* and *Enuies* false surmise,
> Condemned to that Dongeon mercilesse,
> Where they should liue in woe, and die in
> wretchednesse.   (I.v.46)

This vision of the world under the Old Law seen by Langland's Will and by Spenser's knight whose "Will was his guide" (I.ii.12) is combined in both poems with a historical allegory which is found, for example, in the episode of the rats and mice who seek to bell the cat, and in the various trials of Una as the Church. The main drama of the fall is thus set firmly in the poet's own age.

Passus VI–VII : Cantos VI–VII

In Langland the vision of man's fallen state ends with the cry of the repentant who "blustreden forth as bestes ouer bankes and hilles, / Til late was and longe" (v.521–22). In Spenser, Una laments her knight's fall into Orgoglio's dungeon and wanders "long tost with stormes, and bet with bitter wind, / High ouer hils, and low adowne the dale" (I.vii.28). In Langland the repentant folk, when they learn that they can be saved by God who becomes in Christ "owre fader and owre brother," cry upward to Christ "to haue grace to go with hem treuthe to seke" (v.519). In answer to their cry, Piers enters as the instrument of divine grace to lead them to salvation. As the follower of Truth who has gained grace, one who instructs the pilgrims the way to Truth, and later directs them in ploughing his half acre, he prefigures the states of Dowel, Dobet, and Dobest which later are fully manifest in him. Similarly, Arthur enters at the climactic moment as the instrument of divine grace. Now as Una's knight he offers counsel and vows to serve her. As Truth grants condemned mankind a pardon through Piers, Una as Truth guides Arthur to Orgoglio's castle to redeem her fallen knight. In the sermon which heralds Piers' entrance, Repentance reveals that man is saved when God died "in owre sute" and descended into Hell where "thorw the lighte that lepe oute of the lucifer was blent" (v.502). The Red Cross Knight's pardon is represented allegorically through Arthur's battle with Orgoglio. When Arthur's shield is uncovered "such blazing brightnesse through the aier threw" that Orgoglio is defeated and the Dragon "became starke blind" (I.viii.19,20). He enters the castle to make "a deepe descent, as darke as hell, / That breathed euer forth a filthie banefull smell" and there

> with constant zeale, and courage bold,
> After long paines and labours manifold,
> He found the meanes that Prisoner vp to reare.

(I.viii.40)

What Langland asserts as doctrine in the speech of Repentance is presented by Spenser "clowdily enwrapped in Allegoricall deuises."

The rending of the veil of Arthur's shield is the same allegorical moment as Piers' tearing the pardon. Both acts mark the
violent irruption of divine grace into the natural world. In
Spenser that moment comes when the Giant's weapon "heaued
was on hye" to slay the fallen Arthur. "In his fall his shield,
that couered was, / Did loose his vele by chaunce, and open
flew," and its light defeats Orgoglio. In Langland, the priest
impugning the pardon that Truth had sent is the moment of
Piers' total defeat. The Church's denial of the pardon seems to
leave no way open for salvation. At this moment of defeat, Piers
tears it:

> piers for pure tene pulled it atweyne,
> And seyde, *"si ambulauero in medio vmbre mortis,*
> *non timebo mala; quoniam tu mecum es.*
> I shal cessen of my sowyng," quod pieres "and swynk
>   nought so harde,
> Ne about my belly ioye so bisi be namore!"   (vii.116-18)

John Lawlor's remark that "the archetype here pressing upon
the poet is that rending of the veil of the Temple which marked
for ever the end of the Old Covenant and the inception of the
New," [7] applies also to the rending of the veil of Arthur's shield.
The rending in both poems marks the entrance of grace into the
fallen world through which man may be freed from the bondage
of the Law to live under the covenant of Mercy. The "blinde
prieste" (so Crowley terms him), that "lewed lorel" [8] who is
ignorant of the spirit beneath the letter and denies the pardon,
may be compared to Spenser's Ignaro, that aged figure blind and
backward looking, who holds the keys to Orgoglio's castle but

cannot use them. Arthur seizes the keys but finds that they cannot open the iron door which imprisons the knight: by this we understand that the Church of the old dispensation, like the priest, cannot bring salvation to man. When Arthur rends the door open to free the knight he provides him with that pattern of action which Piers provides for the Dreamer. Piers' decision not to be too solicitous about the world awakens in the Dreamer the desire to follow him by learning how to dowel in this world. Finally he becomes the servant of the Samaritan who is Piers who is Christ. Similarly, the Red Cross Knight imitates Arthur when he slays the Dragon which Arthur wounds and suffers the agonies of hell to redeem Una's parents.

Both poems break at this point in a way which has become a crux to our understanding their structure. One Langland critic refers to "that central stumbling-block of *Piers Plowman* interpretation, the connexion between the *Visio* and the *Vita*." [9] Spenser may help to resolve this crux if only because he is a Christian poet writing on the same theme of man's fall and restoration. At that moment when the Red Cross Knight is restored to Una, his pilgrimage truly begins. Up to now he has been Everyman who begins his quest only to fall into sin, where he remains captive until he is restored through God's grace. When he is freed and the same cycle of events may begin again, he realizes Una's faith and Duessa's duplicity. Now his experiences become inwardly illuminating. Similarly for Langland's Dreamer, all that has happened to him prepares him for the moment when he begins his quest. Inevitably both poems break from *Visio* to *Vita:* from a vision of the outer fallen world of good and evil to an inner spiritual pilgrimage which brings regeneration and restoration.

Passus VIII–XII : Canto IX

The second half of each poem opens with a struggle to begin the spiritual pilgrimage and records an inner psychological debate which ends in conversion. Langland's Dreamer wanders in an intellectual maze and wrestles with the "craft[s] in my corps" (1.137)—Thought, Wit, Study, Clergy, and Scripture—in seeking to learn how man may be saved. When he believes in predestination he is scorned by Scripture and falls into an inner vision in which Fortune brings him into the Land of Longing where concupiscence overcomes him. Now becoming aware for the first time of his own sinful state, and being told by Scripture that many are called but few are chosen, he fears damnation:

> Al for tene of her tyxte trembled myn herte,
> And in a were gan I waxe and with my-self to dispute,
> Whether I were chosen or nought chosen;

But at this moment of crisis

> on holicherche I thoughte,
> That vnderfonge me atte fonte for one of goddis chosen;
> For cryste cleped vs alle come if we wolde . . .
> And badde hem souke for synne saufly at his breste,
> And drynke bote for bale brouke it who so myghte.
>
> (XI.110–17)

Then Scripture, a nameless speaker, and Imaginatif equip him for his pilgrimage.

The Red Cross Knight in his weakened state is unable to begin his quest, and during this interlude he meets Despair. The text which causes the Dreamer to wander—*"sepcies in die*

cadit iustus" (viii.21)—is voiced by Despair: "the lenger life, I
wote the greater sin, / The greater sin, the greater punishment"
(i.ix.43). Like the Dreamer, the knight treads an intellectual
maze until, overcome by despair, he too believes in predestination:

> Their times in his eternall booke of fate
> Are written sure, and haue their certaine date.
> Who then can striue with strong necessitie . . .
> Or shunne the death ordaynd by destinie?   (i.ix.42)

He fears damnation; but at this moment of crisis Una as
Holicherche reminds him of God's mercy:

> In heauenly mercies hast thou not a part?
> Why shouldst thou then despeire, that chosen art?
> Where iustice growes, there grows eke greater grace,
> The which doth quench the brond of hellish smart,
> And that accurst hand-writing doth deface.   (i.ix.53)

The faith which Una offers to her despairing knight is that which
is offered to the Dreamer first by Scripture who declares that
"may no synne lette / Mercy alle to amende" (xi.132–33), then
by the speaker who reveals that men live under the law of love
as brothers in Christ (xi.192), and finally by Imaginatif in his
sermon upon God's mercy which brings salvation to all mankind
(xii.268–90).

The Dreamer's intellectual wandering, like the Red Cross
Knight's debate with inner despair, is a necessary prelude to his
pilgrimage. Only through knowledge of his state of damnation
may each turn toward salvation with full faith in God's mercy

to save sinful man. Compared to the Dreamer's wandering, the Knight's meeting with Despair is brief. It is also more intense: the Dreamer records that "al for tene of her tyxte trembled myn herte, / And in a were gan I waxe" while Despair's speech the Knight's "hart did perse . . . whiles trembling horror did his conscience dant, / And hellish anguish did his soule assaile." The difference is to be explained by the Reformation through which the forces of Thought, Wit, Study, Clergy and even Scripture are ranged on the side of Despair while man's individual conscience is burdened by a greater awareness of his depravity under the judgment of God. On the other hand, the firm emphasis upon election and on faith alone as the means to salvation resolves the intellectual debate more quickly.

Vita de Dowel : Canto X

The Dreamer's next vision follows a sharp break in the narrative continuity: after many years of wandering he has cast off his hermit robes and "as a freke that fre were forth gan I walke / In manere of a mendynaunt many a yere after" (xiii.2–3). In a similar action the Red Cross Knight enters the house of Penance where he is despoiled of his armor and becomes a pilgrim. Now as pilgrims the Dreamer and the Knight must undergo penance and purgation of sin. The figures of the Doctor and Haukyn whom the Dreamer meets embody the sins corrupting his flesh. He undergoes a diet of penance until he vows to repent "as long . . . as I lyue and lycame may dure"; then his Conscience, guided by Patience, goes upon a pilgrimage "to mourne for my synnes" (xiii.50, 191). Patience declares that "we shulde nought be to busy a-bouten owre lyflode" (xiv.33), and teaches sinful man what are the "surgienes for dedly synnes" (xɪᴠ.88) : contrition, confession, and satisfaction which

> seketh oute the rote and bothe sleeth and voideth,
> And, as it neuere had ybe to nought bringeth dedly synne,
> That it neuere eft is seen, ne sore but semeth a wounde yheled.
>
> (xɪᴠ.94–6)

The Red Cross Knight, under the teachings of faith, is brought to such perfection that he, too, rejects the active life and repents his sins. As for the Dreamer, Patience the leech heals the root of his ill, "disease of grieued conscience." After he is placed in "a darkesome lowly place" where he undergoes a diet of penance "in him was left no one corrupted iot" (ɪ.x.26).

The pilgrim's next stage is to learn the nature of charity. When the Dreamer asks, "what is charite," Anima teaches him at length the nature of the charitable life. She exhorts "parfit lyuynge" upon "alle that ben at debate and bedemen were trewe" (xᴠ.420). The Red Cross Knight is similarly instructed by Charissa "in euery good behest, / Of loue, and righteousnesse, and well to donne" (ɪ.x.33). As Anima, one who is well-known "in crystes courte . . . and of his kynne a partye" (xᴠ.17) instructs the Dreamer, Mercy "that was both borne and bred / In heauenly throne" (ɪ.x.51) guides the Knight to the holy hospital where "his mortall life he learned had to frame / In holy righteousnesse" (ɪ.x.45).

When the Dreamer is told that Charity grows in the garden of man's heart, he falls into an inner vision of the Tree of Charity upheld by the Trinity and defended by Piers. The Red Cross Knight, being further purified by Contemplation, is caught up in a vision of the heavenly city where the redeemed dwell as Saints with the angels. The Dreamer finds Piers the Plowman within, even as the Knight learns his true nature as one "brought . . . vp in ploughmans state to byde" to become his "owne nations frend / And Patrone" (i.x.61-66). Both visions reveal man's fulfilment in the state of perfection. Coghill argues that the *Vita de Dowel* supplies the moral argument of Langland's poem; and the same may be said of the corresponding section of Spenser's poem. Further, each shows the final inadequacy of the active life and prepares for that higher state in which the Dreamer becomes servant to Piers-Christ and the Knight imitates Christ.

Vita de Dobet : Canto XI

In his search for salvation the Dreamer moves from Faith and Hope to become the servant of the Samaritan-Christ who reveals that only they "and thi-self now, and such as suwen owre werkis" may pass through the wilderness: for the way to salvation is "the weye that ich went and wherforth to iherusalem" (xvii.101, 114). The Dreamer now pursues his way: "I drowe me in that derkenesse to *decendit ad inferna*" where he sees "one semblable to the samaritan & som del to Piers the plowman" (xviii.111, 10) harrowing hell to redeem mankind. The victory of Piers-Christ over Satan and the Red Cross Knight's victory over the Dragon are described in the same apocalyptic terms. First, it reveals the way to man's final regeneration. Earlier, the Dreamer desires to eat Piers' fruit from the Tree of Charity and learns that man may not be saved "tyl he haue eten al the barn [who is Christ] and his blode ydronke" (xvii.97). This assimilation of Christ is shown with his descent into hell where he sees Christ warring in

Piers' arms, *humana natura*. In similar terms, the Knight is
baptized at the Well of Life and anointed by the Tree of Life.
He imitates Christ by recreating Christ within, that is, he becomes Piers-Christ. This final victory also defeats Death: as
Christ descends to slay "the foule fende and fals dome & deth"
(xviii.28), so the Knight meets that fiend who "does his dayly
spoyle" (i.xi.2) and being twice left dead, on the third day rises
to slay Death itself. Inevitably, both poets describe this apocalyptic
battle by the image of light opposing the powers of darkness.
Satan sees where Christ "cometh hiderward seyllynge, / With
glorie & with grete lighte." Through His victory "man shal fro
merkenesse be drawe, / The while this lighte & this leme shal
Lucyfer ablende" (xviii.304–5, 136–37). When the Red Cross
Knight who is one of the "children of faire light" comes to battle
the Dragon, his "glistring armes . . . heauen with light did fill"
(i.xi.4). Finally, the victory redeems all mankind. Through
Christ's victory which releases "Adam & Eue & other moo in
helle" (xviii.176), mankind may be saved. Earlier, Piers tells
the pilgrims that their journey to Truth ends when they reenter
Paradise:

> To wayne vp the wiket that the womman shette,
> Tho Adam and Eue eten apples vnrosted;
> *Paradise porta per euam cunctis clausa est.*
>
> (v.611–13: Crowley, 2d imp.)

Similarly when the Knight slays the Dragon in Eden, Adam
"bad to open wyde his brazen gate" (i.xii.3) and all his people
find peace and joy.

Vita de Dobest : Canto XII

In the final section of Langland's poem, mankind under Piers gains the pardon *redde quod debbes:* "the gode to the godhede & to grete ioye, / And wikke to wonye in wo with-outen ende" (xix.192–93). Though the pardon is the same as before, now the covenant of the Law has been satisfied by Piers-Christ and men live as "gentel men with ihesu" under the dispensation of Mercy. When Piers builds the Barn, "that hous vnite holicherche on englisshe," the Dreamer finally "cam to vnite" (xx.212). The final section of Spenser's poem shows the Red Cross Knight pardoned for serving Duessa through the intercession of Una, and at the end he marries Una. The theme of both endings is man's ultimate restoration: the Dreamer enters Unite which grace has made "in holynesse to stonde" (xix.378) even as the Knight of Holiness marries Una.

Langland's satire concludes with an apocalyptic vision of the coming of Antichrist: through the hypocrisy of the Friars, Unitas is overwhelmed. In contrast, Spenser's heroic poem ends when the hypocrisy of Archimago and Duessa is exposed and Una enjoys "sure peace for euermore" (ii.i.2). In his ecclesiastical level of significance Spenser begins where Langland left off. The defeat of Unitas treats of the wanderings of Una before the Reformation when her earlier defenders were defeated by the Dragon.

> Full many knights aduenturous and stout
> Haue enterprizd that Monster to subdew . . .
> But all still shronke, and still he greater grew:
> All they for want of faith, or guilt of sin,

The pitteous pray of his fierce crueltie haue bin.

(ɪ.vii.45)

The Dragon is defeated only by the coming of her true Champion, Saint George, who represents politically the Protestant power under Elizabeth.

Both poets express the same encyclopedic vision of man's life in the universal terms of fall, redemption through grace, regeneration, and ultimate restoration. Spenser differs where he clarifies Langland. As we have seen, he relegates Langland's satire upon the corrupt Church and worldly prelates to *The Shepheardes Calender*. His greatest change is to divide his matter into the various books. This allows him to confine Langland's digression upon the use of *temporalia* to Book ɪɪ, and problems of civil government to Book v. Thus Langland's vision of Mede becomes many distinct symbols in Spenser: as the foe of Holicherche she appears as Duessa in Book ɪ, as Bribery she is Philotime in Book ɪɪ and later Munera in Book v, and her political significance is shown in Duessa of Book v. This division allows him to reveal Langland's purely religious vision in Book ɪ. Upon the level of anagoge, then, the poems may be seen to correspond as significant analogues.

III

One chief difference between the two poems is seen in their structures. While it is difficult to define the structure of *Piers Plowman,* it may be termed *cumulative:* its slow gathering of significance will suddenly precipitate into the clarity of vision. Spenser's structure is clearly rhetorical. As a Renaissance poet he

wrote within that tradition implicit in Jonson's requirement of
the poet:

> that, which wee especially require in him is an exactnesse
> of Studie, and multiplicity of reading . . . not alone enabling
> him to know the *History*, or Argument of a *Poeme*, and to
> report it: but so to master the matter, and Stile, as to shew,
> hee knowes how to handle, place, or dispose of either, with
> *elegancie*, when need shall bee.[10]

Ever since E.K. praised *The Shepheardes Calender* for being
"well grounded, finely framed, and strongly trussed vp together"
we have been aware of the *elocutio* present in its rhetorical tropes
and schemes. Through the writings of Rosemond Tuve we have
been aware of the importance of *inventio* in his poetry. Yet *The
Faerie Queene* is more radically rhetorical than we allow. In this
section I shall illustrate how the moral argument of Book II is
presented within a rhetorical structure outlined by the seven
traditional parts of *dispositio*. I choose Book II because it is generally held to be merely episodic, assembled rather than planned,
and only partly revised to meet the poet's changing plans. More
precise awareness of Spenser's structure should allow us to define
more clearly the quite different structure of Langland's poem.

It is not surprising that Spenser should use this third part of
rhetoric though it has been noticed only in such prose works as
Sidney's *Apology* and Rainolds' *In Laudem Artis Poeticae*. In a
letter to Gabriel Harvey he speaks of writing a book which "I
dare vndertake wil be . . . rare for the Inuention, and manner of
handling [that is, its disposition]." Since the rhetorical handbooks
describe orations delivered in praise of virtue we may expect

Spenser to avail himself of rhetorical structure in a poem whose
moral argument treats the virtues. Book ɪɪ, especially, lent itself
to classical rhetorical structure, being drawn from the classical
tradition and being, next to Book ᴠ, the most explicitly didactic
and most deliberately framed "to fashion a gentleman or noble
person in vertuous and gentle discipline." In what follows I shall
use Thomas Wilson's *Arte of Rhetorique* because it was the most
influential English rhetorical handbook and offers a full treatment of *dispositio*.

The first part of disposition, the *exordium,* stands apart from
the main body of the work as "the Entraunce or beginning," so
Wilson terms it, which serves to "make [the hearers] vnderstand
the matter . . . with some pleasant tale, or . . . some straunge
thing." [11] The opening episode of Book ɪɪ, Archimago's "ruefull
tale" and Duessa's complaint which so amaze Guyon that in
his error he rashly attacks the Red Cross Knight stands as an
exordium to the moral argument of the Book. It stands apart
from Guyon's quest which begins only after he is blessed by the
Red Cross Knight: then he "must now anew begin, like race to
runne" (ɪɪ.i.32). As an *exordium* it serves to "make [the hearers]
vnderstand the matter" by offering a brief moral allegory of
the book. Guyon is displayed as the image of fallen man who
may be overcome so readily by the intemperate affections. Upon
hearing Archimago's story he "with fierce ire / And zealous hast
away is quickly gone" from the guidance of the Palmer and
"inflam'd with wrathfulnesse" (ɪɪ.i.13, 25) he is ready to attack
the Red Cross. Then the recognition of his error, the firm al-
liance with Holiness which follows his plea for mercy, and the
return of his reason show how man may overcome his intemper-

ate affections. In so displaying the pattern of man's fall into
intemperance and of the means of his restoration the opening
episode becomes a fitting introduction to the book of Temperance.

The *narratio* follows the *exordium,* as Wilson declares: "after
the preface and first Enterance, the matter must be opened, and
euery thing liuely tolde, that the hearers may fully perceiue what
we goe about." In this part writers should reveal the "substaunce"
of their invention and bring "the whole somme of their matter
to one point, that the hearers may better perceiue, whereat they
leuell all their reasons" (pp. 106, 108). Spenser places here the
episode of the bloody-handed Babe which he declares in the
Letter to Ralegh to be his "whole subiect." [12] In Amavia's story
of Mortdant's death through the enchantments of Acrasia, the
matter of intemperance is opened: in her "loues rage" and his
intemperate lust Guyon sees "the image of mortalitie" against
which the Palmer invokes the power of temperance:

> But temperance (said he) with golden squire
> Betwixt them both can measure out a meane,
> Neither to melt in pleasures whot desire,
> Nor fry in hartlesse griefe and dolefull teene.   (ii.i.58)

Then the limitations of temperance are shown in Guyon's vain
efforts to cleanse the Babe's hands. By so revealing the power and
limitations of the virtue for which Guyon fights, and by showing
the nature of intemperance in Mortdant and Amavia, its cause
in Acrasia's Bower of Bliss and its effects in the Babe's bloody
hands, the episode provides a "plaine and manifest pointing of
the matter." [13]

The nature of temperance as the golden mean is defined by

the succeeding episode where Guyon enters the castle of Medina. Her rule over her sisters describes the virtue in Aristotelian terms as the mean between the two extremes of excess and defect, while his battle with the wrathful Huddibras and the lustful Sansloy describes it in Platonic terms as the rational soul divided against the irrational with its subdivisions of the irascible and the appetitive. This "definition" corresponds to the *propositio* which, according to Wilson, comes "straight and immediatly after the Narration" and is "a pithie sentence comprehended in a small roome, the somme of the whole matter" (pp. 111, 7). The temperate state itself is achieved when Medina and Guyon reduce the sisters with their suitors to the state of concord and all gather at a feast.

What the *propositio* defines allegorically as "the somme of the whole matter" is expanded in the episodes from Cantos iv to vii. This section corresponds to the fourth part of rhetorical disposition, the *partitio,* where "the next is . . . to parte out such principall pointes, whereof we purpose fully to debate" (p. 109). Since temperance seeks the harmony of the affections, Guyon's enemy is wrath which brings discord. Wrath is first displayed in Furor aided by Occasion. Though Guyon cannot slay him, the Palmer shows how he may be subdued by binding Occasion. Then Wrath appears in Pyrochles whom Guyon subdues and urges to "fly the dreadfull warre, / That in thy selfe thy lesser parts do moue" (II.v.16). Though subdued by temperance Wrath only seeks occasion to break out again: Pyrochles releases Furor who overcomes him. Wrath also appears in the lustful Cymochles. Against each of these embodiments of wrath Guyon asserts the power of temperance. The final episode of this section, Guyon's passage through Mammon's Cave, demonstrates fully the nature of his virtue. Within the Cave he resists all temptations to fall and proves the virtue for which he fights. Yet at the end he is left helpless before his enemies. This paradoxical outcome demonstrates both the power and limitations of temperance. By the virtue for which he fights he seeks the harmonious mean which includes the extremes. Earlier he could subdue, but not destroy, the irascible and concupiscent passions; now he triumphs only to be defeated by them. At this height and limit of his natural power Arthur enters as the instrument of grace to rescue him.

The rest of the book corresponds closely to the three remaining parts of rhetorical disposition—*confirmatio, confutatio,* and *peroratio*—and may be considered more briefly.

Canto ix begins:

> Of all Gods workes, which do this world adorne,
>> There is no one more faire and excellent,
>> Then is mans body both for powre and forme,
>> Whiles it is kept in sober gouernment;
>> But none then it, more fowle and indecent,
>> Distempred through misrule and passions bace:
>> It growes a Monster, and incontinent
>> Doth loose his dignitie and natiue grace.
>> Behold, who list, both one and other in this place.

The *one,* man's body "kept in sober gouernment" is the house of Alma which Guyon enters to be confirmed in the virtue of temperance. There he gazes with wonder upon its "goodly order, and great workmans skill" which is displayed both in its "wondrous frame" and its "wondrous powre" (II.ix.44, 47). This episode corresponds to the *confirmatio* where, according to Wilson, "wee must heape matter, and finde out arguments to confirme the same to the vttermost of our power, making first the strongest reasons that wee can, and next after, gathering all the probable causes together, that being in one heape, they may seeme strong and of great weight" (p. 112).

The *other,* man's body which through intemperance "growes a Monster, and incontinent / Doth loose his dignitie and natiue grace" is Maleger. His being slain by Arthur is the first part of the *confutatio,* which is "a dissoluing, or wyping away of all such reasons as make against vs" (p. 7). Guyon's triumph over the enchantments of the Bower of Bliss and his binding of Acrasia is the second part of the *confutatio,* the final "dissoluing . . . of all such reasons as make against" the virtue of Temperance.

After the capture of Acrasia and the freeing of her beasts the Palmer moralizes upon the "sad end . . . of life intemperate," and in the concluding stanza of the book both he and Guyon deliver their judgment upon Grill:

> Said *Guyon,* See the mind of beastly man,
>   That hath so soone forgot the excellence
>   Of his creation, when he life began,
>   That now he chooseth, with vile difference,
>   To be a beast, and lacke intelligence.
>   To whom the Palmer thus, The donghill kind
>   Delights in filth and foule incontinence:
>   Let *Grill* be *Grill,* and haue his hoggish mind,
> But let vs hence depart, whilest wether serues and wind.

To the moral argument of Book II this stanza stands as the *peroratio,* "a clarkly gathering of the matter spoken before, and a lapping vp of it altogether." [14] It completes the moral structure of the book—with Canto iii, Braggadocchio's encounter with Belphoebe serving as a formal *digressio*—according to the seven traditional parts of rhetorical disposition.

This moral argument is only one aspect of the structure of Book II. When it is realized in the poetry there is a considerable shift of emphasis: Mammon's Cave and Acrasia's Bower, for example, are given greater significance than the rhetorical structure suggests. Again, it becomes part of a theological structure; and, most important, the whole structure of the Book is elaborately paralleled with the structure of Book I.[15] The more we read Spenser's poem the more we become aware of the centripetal relationship of its parts and how they are deliberately articulated to achieve the unity of the whole poem.

The more precisely we become aware of the structure of Spenser's poem, the more it seems to differ radically from Langland's poem. In one way the structure of *The Faerie Queene* may be considered apart from the content: we speak of its form as heroic or epic or romance, and we trace a particular moral or historical allegory. In short, we see the content within a structure or form. In contrast, the structure of *Piers Plowman* seems to emerge out of its content as though the poem were shaped as the poet was writing. I see its structure deriving in this way from the two opening passus. In the Prologue the Dreamer sees the world around him as it is. To this actual world he responds simply and emotionally: what he sees so clearly he satirizes because of outraged feelings of pity and love. Both the vision and the judgment are given in purely human terms: this is what he sees and how he feels. In Passus I he sees this same world of life upon the order of nature but through Holicherche's

doctrine judges it in terms of what it should be.[16] She shows
him what his first vision "bymeneth": the field is a "mase" poised
between the fall of Lucifer and the fall of love and the busy
folk in it "haue thei worschip in this worlde" (i. 8.). Both the
vision and the judgment are now given in religious terms, and
the Dreamer's response becomes more complex. While he
"knows" the truth which Holicherche tells him, he lacks "kynde
knowing":

"Yet haue I no kynde knowing," quod I "yet mote ye kenne me
    better,
By what craft in my corps it comseth and where.   (1.136–37)

To the world as it should be he responds with his discursive
intellect and what it provides. The tension awakened in him
by the gap between the world as it is and as it should be provides
the argument of the whole poem.

    The poem moves in that area between the satirical and re-
ligious vision of the world. His satire is directed to the end of
refining the evil he sees around him, to reduce it to vision. The
triumph of his vision becomes the climactic moments in the
poem: the vision of the learned Doctor, of Haukyn the *Actiua
Vita,* and finally the figure of Antichrist. When he can project
in himself the evil which he sees in others and leave his will to
become the fool and idiot, his upward quest to save his soul by
knowing Dowel, Dobet, and Dobest becomes a descent into hell.
Then his discursive reason is taken over by the intuitive in his
vision of Piers-Christ harrowing hell. The power of this vision
now illuminates the satire. It allows him in the closing passus
to see the field of fair folk not as poised between the Tower and

the Dungeon, seemingly unaware of both, but locked in a final apocalyptic battle. In the opening vision the Dreamer's satire and Holicherche's doctrine are separate: the final vision includes, and goes beyond, both. In the end is the Dreamer's beginning; only now when Conscience searches for Piers he is armed with a vision. That vision is the poem itself.

The unity of the poem through which we see its structure consists in the relation between the world as it is and as it should be. For the poem is not a spiritual journey, such as *Pilgrim's Progress,* where the pilgrim leaves the world for the Heavenly City. As in Spenser, the vision of the world as it should be prepares for the active life in this world. At the end the Red Cross Knight leaves Una to serve the Faery Queen even as the Dreamer's Conscience seeks Piers. Its unifying vision is neither that of the totally fallen world nor of the redeemed world but rather of the world being harrowed by Piers-Christ. It follows that if we focus upon one world or the other, and consider its social satire or Christian doctrine, we read the work as didactic poetry rather than as a poem. Once we recognize the nature of its unity and see its structure in the relation set up between the Dreamer's two visions of the world, we can treat its "content" as metaphor. At this point it becomes possible to treat the poem as an allegory in relation to Spenser's "continued Allegory, or darke conceit."

IV

To refer to *Piers Plowman* as an allegory may suggest that what the poem tells us on its literal level should be ignored for hidden levels of significance. Nevill Coghill has hinted darkly that the poem's meaning proceeds simultaneously on several different levels. But since the poet expresses his meaning so concretely, some have read the poem as a literal narrative that means no more than what it says. My own view is that we can read it as an allegory which means more than it says only by insisting upon the primacy and integrity of its literal level. Dante suggests this way of reading when he describes the allegory of poets as that in which "the literal sense ought always to come first, as being that sense in the expression of which the others are all included," and when he writes of the allegory of theologians that the highest sense, the anagogic, illuminates and sustains the literal level.[17] More directly Spenser suggests this way of reading, for in his allegory the literal level is primary. His whole effort through his poem is to render clearly defined, exact, and visual images. To strip that literal level away by translating it into other terms leaves the poem barren. Both Dante and Spenser tell "of Forests, and inchantments drear, / Where *more* is meant then meets the ear." [18] We must read the literal level not by translating but by retaining it as metaphor. Then it becomes a radiating center of meaning which organizes whole areas of human experience. If we are to read *Piers Plowman* as an allegory, we need to read it in the same way. Where Spenser differs is in his more deliberate use of fiction which triumphs over any supporting framework of morality and belief. Like Sidney's "right Poet," he "nothing affirmes." [19] In contrast, Langland does seem to affirm truth: what the Dreamer says, for example, has been taken as social satire or Christian doctrine that expresses the poet's view of society or religious belief. Yet in the most recent criticism of the poem we have been made more aware of the *fiction*. We see the Dreamer, for example, as a character who functions within a poetic drama; and since what he "affirms" is expressed chiefly through fragments of himself in Thought and the rest, we are at two removes from simple affirmative statement.

This way of reading the two poems as allegories may be illustrated by considering two comparable episodes, the Dreamer's vision of Piers-Christ harrowing hell and the Red Cross Knight's battle with the Dragon. In *Piers Plowman* the vision merges the various levels of meaning into a final image. The Dreamer's search to know "how I may saue my soule" which forms the literal meaning of the poem is expressed throughout in allegorical terms as the search for the three lives which Piers embodies. The Dreamer learns that the search for Piers is the search to know himself—this is the poem's tropological level of significance —for Charity is within:

> Clerkis kenne me that cryst is in alle places;
> Ac I seygh hym neuere sothly but as my-self in a miroure,
> *Ita in enigmate, tunc facie ad faciem*   (xv.156–58)

and grows in the garden of man's heart, where it is guarded by Piers. When the Dreamer becomes the servant of the Samaritan who is Piers, all the poem's meanings gather upon the level of anagoge into the image of Christ jousting in Piers' armor to redeem mankind. This climactic vision completes the pattern set up in the *Visio*. There the poet assumes the role of an Old Testament prophet crying out upon the abuses of the world. His vision of the world's fallen state heralds the coming of the redeemer, Piers, who is seen in human terms as the good plow-

man through whom mankind may be redeemed. Now all is
fulfilled in the epiphany of Piers: his nature is fully manifest
in the humanity of Christ, and all that he means he is. While this
vision is taken directly from Scripture, the poet has earned it
through his passionate search for Charity. In fact, he precipitates
the coming of Christ through yearning for Piers' fruit. His own
role as a poet is fulfilled for he sees the poet as God's minstrel
who saves souls from Satan by telling "without flaterynge of gode
friday the storye" (XIII.447). In his telling this story it seems as
though the union of God and man has been achieved for the
first time, so completely has the poet rendered the vision his
own. Nevill Coghill writes of his vision: "at last Charity and
Learning, the Good Samaritan and Piers, are made one with
Christ, and He one with humanity. This is (I suppose) the top
of all English allegorical writing, the greatest gathering of the
greatest meanings in the simplest symbols." [20] Fully comparable
is Canto xi, where Spenser with the same kind of imaginative
intensity gathers all the meaning of his poem into a vision of the
Red Cross Knight's three-day battle with the Dragon to free
mankind from prison. Spenser employs the fiction of an armed
knight facing a fire-breathing Dragon while his lady retires to
a hill; but its truth is to be found in its being a metaphor of
Holy Scripture. The Knight's battle in Eden imitates Christ's
harrowing hell and His three-day descent through which mankind is restored to the Well and Tree of Life. His descent is
rendered allegorically: the flames which issue from the Dragon's
mouth whose "deepe deuouring iawes / Wide gaped, like the
griesly mouth of hell" twice cause his fall until on the third day
his weapon pierces that "darksome hollow maw." His victory

frees Adam and Eve from their eternal bondage. The fiction of
both poets, whether given in a historical sense or as romance,
is a metaphor of Holy Scripture.

While the Dreamer's vision of Christ's descent into hell is
given as a literal rendering of Scripture—"and there I saw
sothely *secundum scripturas*" as the Dreamer insists—through
its context in the poem it becomes an imitation of Scripture.
For it is not a vision of Christ as given in Scripture but rather
the poem's vision of Piers-Christ; and even more precisely, it
is the vision of the Dreamer who is the servant of the Samaritan
who is Piers-Christ. While the vision is the climax to all that
has come before, its resolution is given in the four maidens,
Mercy, Truth, Peace, and Righteousness. Their quarrel before
the entrance of the Redeemer expresses all that which had led
the Dreamer on his lengthy pilgrimage. Truth and Righteousness see the world as it is, Mercy and Peace see it as it should
be. When the descent of Christ resolves their quarrel, it purges
the Dreamer. The resolution comes when the Dreamer sees the
four dancing together: "tyl the daye dawed this damaiseles
daunced" (xviii.424). Their ordered movement releases him from
his confused wanderings: from the watching, waiting, kneeling,
running, and descending so that now he is ready to enter
Unitas. Again the only comparable vision is to be found in
Spenser: in Book vi when we penetrate to the sacred nursery of
virtue which inspires the poet we see a hundred naked maidens
"all raunged in a ring, and dauncing in delight" (x.11). Both
poets share the same vision of man's perfected state. Courtesy
becomes a key term in both poems. For Spenser it means "doing
gentle deedes with franke delight" (vi.vii.1) while for Lang-

land it is the "fre liberal wille" (xv.146) which is found in Piers. In both poems we move from the vision of the dancing maidens to the poet himself. From an intensely inward movement the poem suddenly turns outward to embrace the poet's own life. The vision is seen not as an end in itself but preparation for a quest.

The quest defines the form of both poems. The title of Langland's poem in Crowley's editions, "The Vision of Pierce Plowman" may have suggested Spenser's title which is, more exactly, "The Vision of the Faerie Queene" for she appears only in Arthur's vision of her. In the *Letter to Ralegh* Spenser spells out her significance when he relates how Arthur saw "in a dream or vision the Faery Queen": "in that Faery Queene I meane glory in my generall intention, but in my particular I conceiue the most excellent and glorious person of our soueraine the Queene." The Dreamer's quest for Piers is given much the same significance. In both poems the poet's effort to relate this quest to the world around him gives that complexity of structure where —to put it simply—so much goes on that we need to define its form as an allegory.

HARRY BERGER, JR.

A Secret Discipline: *The Faerie Queene,*
Book VI [1]

"Only skilled artists should draw from living bodies, because in most cases these lack grace and good shape."
—TINTORETTO, recorded by Ridolfi

. . . we are told Tintoretto transmuted the gamin divers of the Venetian canals into the angels of his painting. . . . the conquest, in form, of fear and disgust means such a sublimation that the world which once provoked the fear and disgust may now be totally loved in the fullness of contemplation. . . . that gazing . . . is, as Yeats puts it,

 . . . our secret discipline
Wherein the gazing soul doubles her might.
The might is there for the moment when the soul lifts her head.
—R. P. WARREN

THE HELLENISTIC SCHEME for the divisions of the literary treatise —*poesis, poema, poeta*—might be put to rhetorical use as an approach to the dominant movement evident in Spenser's *Faerie Queene. Poesis* adumbrates subject matter, what the poem is about; *poema* refers to questions of form, manner, style, therefore to the imagination in its act of rendering subject matter; *poeta* names the category in which the poet and his conditions are discussed. The increasingly reflexive emphasis articulated by this simple scheme may be transferred to the *Faerie Queene* in the following manner:

1. Books I and II are self-contained, coherent narratives which focus quite clearly on the respective quests of Redcross and Guyon. The allegorical dimension of each book may be shown to have its main purpose in illuminating the character and quest of the fictional hero—the holiness (wholeness) of Redcross and the temperance of Guyon.[2]

2. If in the first two books our attention is directed to the nominal subjects, Books III and IV are presented so as to make us more aware of the act of rendering, the behavior of the poetic mind. In meandering through the places of the classical and courtly landscapes, the romance of Britomart explores both the mythopoetic and the erotic imaginations. The magnificent climaxes of IV.x and IV.xi reveal poetic activity in its most representative aspect, drawing the forms of the mind from oceanic chaos, creating its own symbolic Love and Nature.[3]

3. Books V and VI, though strikingly different from each other, are both unfolded within the ambiance of the poet's contemporary world. They reflect not merely the process of imagination as such, but the problems of the Renaissance poet trying to make sense of the world around him, trying also to continue his interior journey through Faerie amid distractions which make this imaginative quest ever more difficult.

The subject of this essay will be the culmination of this development in the sixth book. Book VI is not, of course, Spenser's final word, but the limits of the topic do not extend to the Mutabilitie Cantos. The essential problem confronting Spenser

in the third phase is defined in the proem to Book v: how to
re-form poetically the corrupt spectacle of modern life in the
ideal images of antiquity. The poet sees that the world around
him is out of joint, and he feels that if he would discharge his
obligation as man and citizen he must try to set it right. Since
the actuality perceived offers no hints of order, no models of
the reality desired, the poetic mind must confer upon the world
its own mythic forms. Spenser's antique forms are those which
he has created in his great poem. The life of his imagination is
compacted into the lives of Artegal, Britomart, and the other
creatures of Faerie. They have their own problems and passions
and destinies, they impose their own claims on their creator.
Although they are make-believe—or precisely *because* they are
make-believe—they are more real to the poet than any of the
fragmented forms he sees in the world outside his mind. And
so, if he is going to make his creatures express that very different
world, he will have to jeopardize their independence. Justice,
as he remarks in the tenth canto, "Oft spilles the principall, to
save the part." And the same holds true for an allegory of
justice: the "principall" is the concrete world of adventure, the
"part" the allegorical or exemplary meaning. But this is not
merely a problem facing the poet: he makes it his theme—no
doubt, if Josephine Bennett's chronology is right, his revision of
Book v was governed by this reflexive awareness. The body
of the poem is always threatened with the fate of Munera, the
Lady Meed figure in Canto ii. Munera has fair locks and a
slender waist, but she also has gold hands and silver feet. Talus
nails up her symbolic extremities and throws the rest of her in
the river. Though Artegal is momentarily moved by her femi-

ninity, he does not interfere. The allegory of justice requires
that when a particular episode is over, its apposite meaning be
nailed up on the wall, and its remaining details discarded.

Book vi should be understood as the logical result of these
developments. It is at once an attempt to cope with justice at
the personal and social levels, and to give freer play to the
stylistic reflexes of the poet's imagination. In accordance with
these needs, the chivalric idiom must be more emblematic, the
view of actuality more oblique. To move from justice to courtesy
means to turn away from the direct and rigorous moral con-
frontation of Book v toward the more mannered and esthetic
perspective of Book vi. This accords with one of the poem's
compositional rhythms: Books i, iii, and v are mainly British
books because they are, in different ways, approaches to the real
or the actual—as theological, as natural, as social. But Books
ii, iv, and vi seem to involve corresponding withdrawals into
Faerie. Book v presents the decay of antique norms, and the
threatened subjection of Spenser's antique forms, before the
darkness of the present. Book vi retreats from the plains, moun-
tains and rocky coast of Book v into the rich wood of Faerie
forms and motifs.

Space does not allow a close inquiry into the effects of the
transition on the sixth book. But a brief listing of its main
features may suggest something of its quality. There is, for
example, a deliberate casualness in Spenser's treatment of narrative and character. After the first canto almost every episode is
left unresolved: the poet breaks off an incident promising further
installments which never materialize;[4] or he presents a situation
whose very nature is inconclusive, as in the case of Mirabella;[5]

or he conclusively ends an episode before our narrative expecta-
tions have been fulfilled, as with Priscilla, Serena, and Pastorella.[6]
This effect is impressed on us by the heavily stressed transition
from one story to another.[7] At times he introduces details and
motifs of romance which are left undeveloped, and made to
flaunt their irrelevance, as in the story told by Matilda to
Calepine.[8]

The characters are all flat and typical, and it is often hard to
keep them straight. This is made worse by a similarity in names
and situations: the same *kinds* of situation recur again and again,
and the poet merely substitutes one set of figures for another.
There is, however, a pattern in the substitutions, for the second
group is always worse or more ineffective than the first—we
move from Crudor to Turpine, from Calidore to Calepine, from
the hermit to Melibee, from the noble savage to the cannibals to
the bandits. As a result, we are aware of a progressive flawing
in the romance world. Related to this pattern are the wounds
inflicted by the blatant beast, which grow steadily worse and do
not respond to physical treatment.[9] Physical action, in general,
is played down. The problems posed by courtesy and slander
pertain to the sting infixed in the name, not in the body. The
physical action demanded by the chivalric idiom is revealed as
inadequate—both in its narrative and its symbolic functions.

Though variety is stressed by the transitions and large number
of episodes, the poet continually returns to a small number of
motifs. There are the motifs of the nursery,[10] the gifts of nature,[11] the foundling; [12] the motif of withdrawal and return,
or of retirement; [13] the motif of primitivism, related to the
nursery theme and diversely embodied in the savage, the can-

nibals, and the shepherds. There is the motif of the center and
the ring which appears in three progressively higher and more
symbolic stages: Serena at the raised altar surrounded by cannibals; Pastorella on a hill surrounded by swains; and the un-
named figure on Mount Acidale surrounded by dancing graces.
The most frequently repeated motif is, significantly enough, that
of a character surprised in a moment of diversion.[14] Such
moments are all perfectly natural or necessary—love, sleep, hunt-
ing, or merely a walk in the woods. These are the small but
precious joys of everyday life, and they are not the ordinary
subjects of the epic world. Yet to these moments the poet adds
many touches which might be called homely or realistic—the
care of babies, the adjustment of harness and pasturing of
mounts, the gathering of food and other agricultural details.[15]
This realistic texture keeps the actual world always before us,
even in the heart of Faerie. Precisely here, where we feel most
secure, where we momentarily turn our backs on the outside
world, the danger is greatest. For the beast of slander is no
chivalric figure. The hermit, who knows this, gives hard counsel
to Timias and Serena: "Abstain from pleasure, restrain your
will, subdue desire, bridle loose delight, use scanted diet, for-
bear your fill, shun secrecy and talk in open sight" (vi.7, 14).
In other words, "Keep your eye always on the treacherous world
around you; don't withdraw, don't relax, for a single moment."

The result of these features is curiously ambivalent. The poet
is bemused, a little bewildered, by the rich variety of Faerie, its
many paths, the lure of so many joys: the opening stanzas of the
proem and the final stanza of the sixth book together suggest
that he is like all the lovers in the woods, or Timias with Bel-

phoebe, or Arthur distracted by thoughts of Gloriana (vii.6).
At the same time, the hermit's advice embodies an element of
awareness in the poet which is responsible for the stylistic traits
just described. The contrivance of the narrative, the inconclusive-
ness of the adventures, the gradual flawing of the romance world,
the failure of chivalric action—these dramatize the claims imposed by actuality on the life of imagination. They also reveal the
poet's awareness that the problems of life cannot be solved by
poetry, cannot even be adequately represented in the simplified
forms of Faerie. J. C. Maxwell has remarked that Spenser's
handling of certain episodes "betrays a mind not fully engaged
by what it is doing." [16] This is meant as criticism, but it is
likely that Spenser intended it as a poetic effect: he *shows*
poetry facing the actual world to cope with the difficult social
problems of slander and courtesy, but he *knows* poetry's true
work and pleasure require detachment rather than involvement.
Something of this attitude is written into his curious presentation of the blatant beast.

The beast is an emblem or symbol which is clearly distinguished from the thing symbolized, so that the complex rela-
tions of slander and courtesy are reduced to an artificial and
ideographic fable. Calidore thinks he is chasing some sort of
animal possessed of two unfriendly habits: it bites and it re-
viles.[17] The first is a shorthand version of the effects of the
second, and it permits the evil to be expressed in physical terms
so that chivalric action is possible. This is a radically reduced
image of the social dangers disclosed toward the end of Book v,
and of a profound spiritual evil with which Spenser was pre-
occupied throughout his career. The blatant beast, as I have

suggested elsewhere,[18] embodies the social expression of the malice produced by despair and self-hatred—the despair of the have-not who hungers after the good of others, who sees himself deprived of place and function, totally dependent on the world outside him, stripped of any "daily beauty in his life." The words of Slander in Book IV, of Envy, Detraction, and the "raskall many" in Book V are uttered to alleviate inward pain rather than to express meanings; their words become a form of rending, a spiritual cannibalism whose perverse and irrational music is aimed at the nerves and the affections:

> Her words were not, as common words are ment,
>   T'expresse the meaning of the inward mind,
>   But noysome breath, and poysnous spirit sent
> From inward parts, with cancred malice lind,
> And breathed forth with blast of bitter wind;
>   Which passing through the eares, would pierce the hart,
>   And wound the soule it selfe with griefe unkind:
> For like the stings of Aspes, that kill with smart,
> Her spightfull words did pricke, and wound the inner part.
>   (IV.viii.26)

The emblematic descriptions of the blatant beast (i.7–9, vi. 9–12, xii.26–28) adumbrate this evil and suggest the rich complexity of meaning packed into the image. The bite then brings all this to bear on a character in such a way as to compare the peculiarly simplified existence of Faerie creatures with the difficulties of actual victims. Since slander in real life is not conveniently gathered together into the form of a single monster, and since—as the hermit points out (vi.6–7, 13–14)—the sting infixed in the name is not susceptible of physical remedies, Calidore's pursuit and conquest can hardly be anything but wish fulfillment.

This is in fact the way the final battle is presented: the affair is purely literal, and the beast is diminished not only from an emblem to an unsymbolic animal, but also from a fearful monster to little more than a muzzled cur. Thus, after a terrifying pre-battle bristle in which it bares a jaw crammed with significance (xii.26–28), it responds to Calidore's attack by "rearing up his former feete on hight" and ramping "upon him with his ravenous pawes" (xii.29). As Spenser cuts the contest down to size, hero and enemy are compared to a butcher and bull in the abattoir (xii.30), and the beast then behaves like an angry girl: "almost mad for fell despight, / He grind, hee bit, he scratcht, he venim threw" (xii.31). Compared to this, the epic similes look clearly oversized and are deliberately misapplied to stress disparity rather than likeness (xii.32, 35). While the Hydra's thousand heads increase in stanza 32, the tongues of the waning beast diminish from a thousand (i.9, xii.27) to the hundred he originally owned when he offered Artegal a glancing threat (v.xii.41, vi.xii.33). Finally, Calidore applies a muzzle and a "great long chaine" and draws him trembling "like a fearefull dog" through Faerie. The conclusion of the quest has nothing to do with slander, everything to do with an Elfin hero's dream: it is a ticker-tape parade through Faerie, whose crowds "much admyr'd the Beast, but more admyr'd the Knight" (xii.38)— the most triumphant and ridiculous of all Elfin homecomings, exposed a moment later when the beast roars into the present and threatens the poet. Thus, as an allegorical creature, given a shape and a place in the poem, the complex evils summarized in the term slander can be understood and controlled. But they can only be controlled in the play world created by the mind. What the beast represents is still in the actual world, and not in a simply identifiable form but diffused among the corrupt, weak, and bitter spirits of civilization.

The importance of courtesy is dialectically illuminated by this danger. Maxwell has indicated the allegorical irrelevance of the beast's relationship to its victims,[19] and this irrelevance constitutes its meaning: attacks of slander are not made on the evil but on the virtuous, otherwise they would not be slander. Since the beast represents nothing whatsoever in the souls of its victims, its forays appear as sudden and inexplicable to us as they do to the sufferers. The armor of courtesy consists of "outward shows" which fulfill rather than deceptively conceal "inward thoughts." It is not simply *a* virtue, nor merely an ornamental polish distinguishing gentry from boors, but a technique of survival in a difficult world; courtesy makes virtue and virtuous behavior possible, maintains trust between men, keeps open the lines of civilized communication. Actuality, with its dangers, requires a movement out from the virtuous center to the circumference of the self where others are met. But—and this is the trouble for the poet who must exercise this technique even in poetry—such a movement diametrically opposes the poet's tendency to journey inward toward the mind's center, toward the source of his ravishing gift.

Thus the apparent inattention noted by Maxwell seems deliberate, and springs from a conflict which lies at the heart of Spenser's work. On the one hand, poetry is his supreme pleasure;

on the other hand he has to survive; especially if he is a pro-
fessional dependent on patronage, his delight must be tempered
to his needs and those of others. Circumstances force the poet as
man to adapt his poetry to the actual environment. But the man
as poet is concerned with his second nature, the world within
the poem, a world of which he is creator and legislator. If poetry
is play, it is deadly serious play, a way of life in which imaginary
experience means more than actuality—Spenser is thoroughly
Neoplatonist in his belief that the soul can turn inward and find
a second world more perfect and real than the first. But he is
also aware of the mind's limits: in a negative sense, the limits
placed *on* the imaginary by the actual; in a more positive sense,
the limits *of* the imaginary. For if the muses transport him to an
ideal world perfected by wish or perverted by nightmare, will they
not reward him with a glimpse of the real? Will they render him
defenseless against the threats of the beast, or deny the actual
world its own rightful claims on a man's inner life? If they ravish
him, are they sirens or something better?

Questions of this sort had been raised by Spenser as early as
The Shepheardes Calender, and they are raised again in the
proem to Book VI. They are implicit in the three modes of
pastoral whose names were given, and distinctions blurred, by
E.K.—*recreative, moral,* and *plaintive* may be understood more
literally than his discussion indicates. Recreative pastoral is a
poetry of escape in a holiday world free from care: its swains
use the problems of life as excuses for indulging in song; delight-
ing chiefly in rhetoric and the manipulation of *topoi,* they pursue
their bent both for its own sake and for its social value as en-
tertainment. In Colin's *April* song of Eliza, for example, the

mythic figures are nothing more than names—adjectives rather
—applied as ornaments to the Queen. The richness of tradition
and meaning which makes one mythic figure distinct from another has been rigorously screened out of the poetry; it appears
only in E.K.'s gloss where much of it (*e.g.,* the Three Graces,
Ap. 267-274) will remain until April is revisited on Acidale.

The moral eclogues are mainly about the inadequacy of the
artless to verbalize or clearly reflect on the problems of the great
world—behind these eclogues one feels the force of the Ciceronian
commonplace about wisdom and eloquence both being necessary
to hold civilization together. The moral pastors, who live in the
English countryside rather than England's Helicon, lack control
of thought and expression, are sadly wanting in the poetic,
dialectical, and rhetorical disciplines necessary to proper communication. These eclogues argue the ethical function of poetic
skill. The great world *is* corrupt, and this is the problem: someone has to deal with it. Someone needs the knowledge, the
shrewdness, the sophistication, the command of expression to
cope with the evils and articulate them with clarity. In the great
world, knaves seize power by playing roles and practising the
arts of persuasion, therefore—since the moral pastor is too simple, perhaps too honest, certainly too lazy—poets are enjoined to
fulfill their social obligations: the esthetic pleasure must not be
channeled into escape and mere recreation, but placed in the
service of the public good.

Thus the recreative and moral modes appear incompatible and
incomplete as displayed in the *Calender:* the former turns away
from life to poetry, the latter from poetry to a sort of life. The
plaintive eclogues are quite simply complaints. They center on

Colin's skill and, with the exception of the November eclogue, on his love, though their rhetoric shades the meaning into a variety of other problems. As the title of Spenser's later volume suggests, the term *complaints* comes to cover any sort of frustration or disappointment with actual life and the human condition —"death, or love, or fortunes wreck" (*Epithalamion* 8). Colin is a recreative shepherd whose art has been cut short by a love which, since it keeps him from poetry, breaks all pastoral rules. He is unlike the moral pastors not only because he embodies rhetorical culture—his personality is compacted of *topoi*—but also because he was first moved by the joy of poetry; he is unlike the recreative pastors because his problem goes beyond the limits of his poetry. Therefore he provides Spenser with a possible way out of the recreative-moral dilemma. This way has two related characteristics: (1) it involves frustration, withdrawal, and the ideal re-creation of life in imaginary forms; (2) it is committed to literary and cultural commonplaces—the treasures of the muses —as the raw materials of poetic style, the traditional seeds which will germinate in the soil of personal experience. It is the way which, as we know, leads to Mount Acidale.

The proem to Book vi begins with an expression of the recreative impulse, though at a much deeper level than in the earlier work. The first two stanzas, after all, follow the moral and plaintive poetry of Book v:

> The waies through which my weary steps I guyde,
>   In this delightfull land of Faery,
>   Are so exceeding spacious and wyde,
>   And sprinckled with such sweet variety,

Of all that pleasant is to eare or eye,
That I nigh ravisht with rare thoughts delight,
My tedious travell doe forget thereby;
And when I gin to feele decay of might,
It strength to me supplies, and chears my dulled spright.

Such secret comfort, and such heavenly pleasures,
Ye sacred imps, that on Parnasso dwell,
And there the keeping have of learnings threasures,
Which doe all worldly riches farre excell,
Into the mindes of mortall men doe well,
And goodly fury into them infuse;
Guyde ye my footing, and conduct me well
In these strange waies, where never foote did use,
Ne none can find, but who was taught them by the Muse.

The muses make him forget his tedious "travell": not only the labor of art but perhaps also the straight and difficult path dictated by such a purpose as the allegory of Justice. They tempt him from the goal, lead him the long way round, and yet refresh the goal-bound spirit. The imagination recognizes both the risk and the privilege of so profound a holiday diversion: it cannot find this ideal place unless the muse reveals, but it may lose its way in Faerie unless the muse leads it out. The muses are felt to be an independent and objective power, an ambiguous *Other* imposing on his will. The poet's problem is the same as Arthur's when he was lured into a new world by his dream of Gloriana: he has to find out "whether dreames delude, or true it were" (1.ix.14). The presence of the muses within him demands a response of will: it is man who must put them to the test, whose experience or experiment will discover and articulate their divinity.

Spenser's response in stanzas 3 and 4 of the proem is an attempt to keep the muses honest. He asks for moral illumination as well as pleasure: "Revele to me the sacred noursery / Of vertue." From the fourth to the sixth stanza he poses then rejects the temptation to withdraw completely from the corrupt world around him, to go straight to "vertues seat . . . deepe within the mynd, / And not in outward shows, but inward thoughts defynd." At the end of the proem he acknowledges a source of virtue at the center of the social order in the person of the divinely appointed Queen: "Right so from you all goodly vertues well / Into the rest, which round about you ring." This is the first instance of the geometric motif which will be repeated three times in the poem, and it is the only case in which the dynamic image is discerned in forms that inhabit real nature; the others are Faerie rings discovered or devised "deepe within the mynd."

The significance of these two kinds of circle, actual and imaginary, becomes clearer if we recall a familiar element of Plotinian thought utilized by Ficino and other Renaissance Neoplatonists: the notion that when the objective Idea proceeds downward from the World Mind to the World Soul and Nature it may divide into two forms of existence, actual and mental. The Idea may be incarnated in the form of one human being and may exist as a form or concept in the mind of another. The mental form is purer than its incarnate analogue and may be aroused by it—this is the more or less utilitarian function of the beloved in Neoplatonist love psychology. In terms of Book vi, the geometrical symbol represents an objective *harmonia* which God has embodied in the Queen and her order, and the muses have implanted in the poetic imagination. Elizabeth's circle will be transfigured on Mount Acidale; when its full richness and meaning are unfolded it will be understood as one of many embodiments of that single form gathered together through the quest of imagination, through the reversion of the mind from the scattered particulars of experience to the Idea which is their formal source. Thus on Acidale the center is, so to speak, pushed upward so that it is the apex of a spiral or a mountain top.

II

The episodes leading up to Mount Acidale center on Faerie figures drawn from the realm of literary conventions: Mirabella, the Proud Fair of Petrarchan fame; Serena, the Distressed Maiden of romance, whose name seems as deliberate an irony as her antiromantic encounter with the cannibals; Pastorella, the aristocratic foundling who presides over the idyllic community of recreative and moral pastors. Each of these episodes constitutes an evocation of an ideal (as opposed to actual) community, completely unified and controlled by the mind, and each is a self-contained environment, a circle focused on its conventional center. Mirabella, surrounded by "murdered" lovers, gives way to the antithetical image of Serena about to be murdered; the raw nature of the cannibals, remote ancestors of the rending beast, is replaced by the "raw" artifice of walking pastoral commonplaces. Mirabella projects the germinal form of frustration, Serena and her cannibals the germinal form of desire, Pastorella and her

swains the germinal form of poetic recreation, all of which are
infolded and transfigured by Colin's vision. Each, then, is a kind
of beginning, an apparent but not a real nursery, a primitive
version of that ravishing source finally discovered deep within
the mind. And each is centered on a female figure who adumbrates the source or object of desire, the cause or effect of a certain mode of imagination. Each figure, that is, embodies claims
on the male psyche that seem to be imposed by some outside
force, some otherness working in or through the form of woman.

Like other incidents in Book VI, the Mirabella episode
(vii.27–viii.30) has the air of being a reprise: in a kind of miniature compass it recalls the erotic atmosphere of Books III and IV
(especially Busirane's house), the Cruel Fair sonnets among the
Amoretti, passages from *Colin Clouts Come Home Againe* and
the *Hymne of Love.* This is the world of erotic narcissism and
courtly love where, as C. S. Lewis has shown, all human activity
is subordinated to the consciousness of desire. Love becomes art,
war, religion, a way of life, and a form of death. In the Court
of Cupid *topos* (vii.32–37) Spenser presents a totally artificial
world which, with its carefully sustained legal metaphor, smacks
of oversophistication. Like Busirane's tapestry, the imagination
by displaying its gold thread asserts the power of art over hap-
hazard nature.

Mirabella is a typical projection of the Petrarchan lover's im-
patience, a scapegoat for his lust—not the image of a real woman
so much as a single aspect of the feminine psyche abstracted and
personified as a Faerie creature—like Belphoebe, Florimell,
Amoret. The Mirabellan frustration produces a desire which
gradually obsesses and paralyzes the will, so that the decadent

refinements and rituals of Cupid are means by which the natural processes of love and life are suspended, the condition of lust fixated rather than sublimated. The source of this fixation which Spenser has so exhaustively explored is suggested in viii.28–29: Mirabella's "meane parentage and kindred base"—we think momentarily of Rosalind—are related to the "wondrous giftes of natures grace" which made all men admire her. This is simply her physical beauty, the first gift of nature. Since she lacks the second gift of spirit, her popularity reflects on the love entertained by her suitors: "Yet was she lov'd of many a worthy pere, / Unworthy she to be belov'd so dere." Theirs is the first undisciplined response to beauty; its aim is physical satisfaction, immediate union rather than sustained *com*munion. It is this longing which has produced Mirabella—all Mirabellas—and given her the power to tyrannize the male appetite. Her name means Beauty-look, beautiful-looking, or perhaps Beauty-mirror: not the true beauty but a physical image, not her own but a reflection of the beholder's passion. Like the Eros of Plato's *Symposium,* she is born of poverty and plenty—the poverty of lust and the plenty of nature's gifts.

This evil is connected to the more general theme of the need for alertness, the threat of actuality which led the hermit to warn the beast's victims, "First learne your outward sences to refraine / From things, that stirre up fraile affection" (vi.7). Lovers must be inwardly alert, their first sight demands temperance by insight if it is to lead to that second sight which is *re*-spect. And in the *Hymne of Beautie,* Spenser describes this insight in Neoplatonic terms which connect it to the poetic process:

> all that like the beautie which they see,
> Streight do not love: for love is not so light,
> As streight to burne at first beholders sight.
>
> But they which love indeede, looke otherwise,
> With pure regard and spotlesse true intent,
> Drawing out of the object of their eyes,
> A more refyned forme. . . .   (ll. 208–214)

First sight is the passive response to the gifts of physical nature, the sensory signals from actuality. In its context, the Mirabella episode connects her with the inability to transform first sight by insight. If we recall Colin's problem in the *Calender*, we may add to the charges against Mirabella the fact that she even stops the recreative pleasure of poetry. True poetry, like true love, cannot proceed until Mirabella has been controlled or transformed by creative insight, and it is significant that Spenser visualizes, exposes, and exercizes Mirabella before moving toward Colin's vision on Acidale. One may see the episode as the poet's way of taking his revenge out on an image; but one may also see the whole movement from Mirabella to Acidale as a poet's progress reunderstood, a transition from the wound to the bow.

Serena's character and predicament are diametrically opposed to Mirabella's. Here, the men are the aggressors, and what they project on the helpless object is a primitive confusion of hunger, lust, and ritual awe. Yet the cannibal and Petrarchan lovers are shown to have something in common:

> they hands upon her lay;
> And first they spoile her of her jewels deare,

> And afterwards of all her rich array;
> The which amongst them they in peeces teare,
> And of the pray each one a part doth beare.
> Now being naked, to their sordid eyes
> The goodly threasures of nature appeare:
> Which as they view with lustfull fantasyes,
> Each wisheth to him selfe, and to the rest envyes.
>
> Her yvorie necke, her alablaster brest,
>   Her paps, which like white silken pillowes were,
>   For love in soft delight thereon to rest;
>   Her tender sides, her bellie white and clere,
>   Which like an Altar did it selfe uprere,
>   To offer sacrifice divine thereon;
>   Her goodly thighes, whose glorie did appeare
>   Like a triumphall Arch, and thereupon
> The spoiles of Princes hang'd, which were in battel won.
>   (viii.41–42)

Serena's "goodly threasures of nature" are detailed in a typical sonneteer's catalogue in which the Lady is parceled out into a number of valuable minerals or vegetables. More striking than the difference between primitive and civilized responses is the similarity: Cupid's poet-lovers have progressed far in ornamental refinements, little in true spiritual culture. Both primitive and civilized lovers respond to the same stimulus, for the savages are aroused by Serena's beautiful face "Like the faire yvory shining" (viii.37).

  In the catalogue Serena becomes an anatomy of love, religion, and war, a cradle or epitome of civilization. This may suggest the continuity of urges and difference of expression between the two societies; an analogy is provided by the relation of the inarticulate Noble Savage to the courtly hero. Seen this way, culture is the only natural environment for man, the full flowering of mind into a social order redeemed from raw actuality. But if one thinks of Cupid's world, where love is a religion and warfare as well as a "soft delight," the restraints imposed by society may be seen to cause the most elaborate and widely diffused corruption of spirit. The female body becomes the source of all value, the object of all desires—we may recall the troubador's *mi dons* and the kind of idolatry on which Mirabella capitalized ("What could the Gods doe more, but doe it more aright?").

Spenser's cannibals provide a physical image the very form of which exposes both the evils treated in the sixth book and the source of actual disorder which jeopardizes the poetic imagination. The savages do not take a stand within themselves or stay in one place to cultivate, to impose a form on experience; and like Mother Hubberd's knaves, they wander about on the borders, encroach on the beings of others:

> There dwelt a salvage nation, which did live
> Of stealth and spoile, and making nightly rode
> Into their neighbors borders; ne did give
> Themselves to any trade, as for to drive
> The painefull plough, or cattell for to breed,
> Or by adventrous marchandize to thrive;
> But on the labours of poore men to feede,
> And serve their owne necessities with others need.
>
> (viii.35)

In their urge to rend and devour, to serve their own necessities, they reveal the evil of the blatant beast in its unsublimated character. Crudor, the Noble Savage, and the other artificial versions of the evil or the primitive give way to an image in which both manner and subject pretend to lack of imaginative refinement. The episode appears as a kind of bedrock, an etiological account which strips away the veneer of civilization.

But as a myth of origins, the cannibals reveal something else. They are not entirely free of restraint, and the appearance of Serena produces a first response of withdrawal. The priest rebukes their lust, advising them

> not to pollute so sacred threasure,
> Vow'd to the gods: religion held even theeves in measure.
>
> So being stayd, they her from thence directed
> Unto a little grove not farre asyde,
> In which an altar shortly they erected,
> To slay her on . . .
>
>   .   .   .   .   .
>
> Of few green turfes *an altar soone they fayned,*
> And deckt it all with flowers, which they nigh hand obtayned.
>   (viii.43–44, italics mine)

It is an ironic, even a comic, withdrawal, yet "fayned" points the way from the body's altar toward the temple and the mind. Though Spenser remarks that they found Serena "by fortune blynde" (viii.36), the cannibals think, because of her beauty, that she was sent by "heavenly grace" (viii.37). Serena is still a thing and not a person, an object and not an Other, an It and not a

Thou. But she has already begun to be a symbol for the cannibals, whose crude religion is shown to be no less indigenous than lust and hunger. They are confused by this adumbration of the divine, and they do not know how to respond to it. The priest, functioning in his Orphic role as an Ur-poet, directs them to an act of ritual imagination, *i.e.,* it is better to murder Serena on God's behalf than rape her on their own.

Spenser's cannibals strike all sorts of Freudian sparks, but they are better understood in the light of the Neoplatonic psychology elaborated by Ficino. It will be useful briefly to indicate the points of doctrine relevant to Spenser's erotic and poetic psychology: Beauty is the visible manifestation of God's goodness as it radiates outward from the divine center through the four cosmic circles of Creation; it produces Ideas in Mind, Concepts in Soul, Seeds in Nature, and Shapes in Matter.[20] Perception begins with shapes, the images of material objects; then, moving inward and upward, it corrects these by reference to Ideas (formulae), innate though germinal forms which the mind unfolds through experience and in the activity of thought.[21] "Since human thought rises from the senses,[22] we invariably judge the divine on the basis of what seems to us highest in physical bodies." Yet the shapes of bodies "neither sufficiently are divine things, nor adequately represent them to us, for the true things are the Ideas, Concepts, and Seeds."[23] The Neoplatonic quest is a reversion to the divine source, a recovery within the forms of human consciousness of the creative principle. Seen in this light, the love of Mirabella is regressive, for her beauty attracts neither to God nor to her soul but outward and "downward" to her body. Spenser's transition to the cannibal ring logically reduces the sophisticated evil to its confused origin and, in effect, allows him to begin all over again:

> it happens that the passion of a lover is not quenched by the mere touch or sight of a body, for it does not desire this or that body, but desires the splendor of the divine light shining through bodies, and is amazed and awed by it. For this reason lovers never know what it is they desire and seek, for they do not know God Himself. . . . . . Hence it also happens that lovers somehow both worship and fear the sight of the beloved. . . . It also often happens that the lover wishes to transform himself into the person of the loved one.[24]

What the mind seeks is not what it finds in the actuality of Matter and Nature, but what it finds deep within itself, what it creates and expresses as culture in its attempt to envisage the divine as it can. The savages have nothing but a woman on which to project their primitive *eros,* and the Petrarchan catalogue describing Serena suggests that their *eros* demands new objects, different modes of expression, more refined forms. However obscure, the primitive *eros* is the response to God which the Neoplatonists call love, "the desire of beauty." It is a desire which involves not only passive pleasure, not only the urge for generation in nature, but also the urge to create, in Diotima's words, "that which is proper for the soul to conceive or contain," *i.e.,* wisdom and virtue. "And such creators are poets and all artists who are deserving of the name inventor" (*Symposium* 209, Jowett trans.). The soul is driven by its very confusion before the poverty of the actual—the mere gifts of nature—to create the symbolic forms which embody its desire and shadow its goal; objectifying these forms into an environment it may better understand its own energy by gazing at its diverse cultural images. Therefore, *eros* produces a cultural dialectic between the soul and its environment: each soul is born into a world of institutions, traditions, and conventions which are external to it and impersonal, yet which are the work of previous souls; they supply the vocabulary through which the soul defines its desire, the forms through which it articulates its experience. The soul internalizes these forms, makes them personal, makes them new.

But if "making it new" proceeds by that sculptural Michelangelesque energy which R. P. Blackmur has called the "inward mastery of experience," it is sustained by delight; its original motive is recreation and play. And this accounts for the transition from the primitive to the rustic nursery in the ninth canto. The description of Pastorella and her circle echoes that of Serena and hers:

> Of few greene turfes an altar soone they fayned,
> And deckt it all with flowres, which they nigh hand
>   obtayned.

> Tho when as all things readie were aright,
>   The Damzell was before the altar set,
>   Being alreadie dead with fearefull fright.   (viii.44–45)

> Then gan the bagpypes and the hornes to shrill,
>   And shrieke aloud, that with the peoples voyce
>   Confused, did the ayre with terror fill,

And made the wood to tremble at the noyce:
The whyles she wayld, the more they did rejoyce.

(viii.46)

A few stanzas later we meet Pastorella, wearing a crown

Of sundry flowres, with silken ribbands tyde,
Yclad in home-made greene that her owne hands
    had dyde.

Upon a little hillocke she was placed
    Higher then all the rest, and round about
    Environ'd with a girland, goodly graced,
    Of lovely lasses, and them all without
    The lustie shepheard swaynes sate in a rout,
    The which did pype and sing her prayses dew,
    And oft rejoyce, and oft for wonder shout,
    As if some miracle of heavenly hew
Were downe to them descended in that earthly vew.

And soothly sure she was full fayre of face,
    And perfectly well shapt in every lim,
    Which she did more augment with modest grace,
    And comely carriage of her count'nance trim,
    That all the rest like lesser lamps did dim:
    Who her admiring as some heavenly wight,
    Did for their soveraine goddesse her esteeme,
    And caroling her name both day and night,
The fayrest Pastorella her by name did hight.

(ix.7–9)

Pastorella is later revealed as an aristocrat, a true Faerie heroine.
As the center of rustic and recreative pastoral, she symbolizes

the artificial desire on which it is based—the escape to the *Petit-Trianon*. It is an existence sustained by the act of naming, the pleasure of words and song. Pastorella's fairy-tale return to her noble parents suggests the continuity of Spenser's earlier and later, his lower and higher, recreative forms.

In naming her, the swains reduce her from an aristocrat to a shepherdess; in worshiping her, they exalt her from an aristocrat to a goddess, identifying the symbol with the reality to which it refers. In this way the essential limits of the pastoral idyll are defined: a simplified paradise whose narrow confines are exalted by its inhabitants to a perfect world complete with incarnate divinity. Its philosopher gives low marks to aspiration and un-fulfilled desire, preaching that very sufficiency of the first nature which the sixth book questions. Melibee's "morality" is in fact the same kind of excuse for laziness used by the moral pastors of the *Shepheardes Calender;* it is a recreative withdrawal from care.[25] In the recreative situation the manner, the manipulation of the medium, the present activity, becomes an end in itself, and what looks like symbolism may only be an excuse for indulging in the self-sufficient pleasures of play.

But it is precisely this pleasure which will lead to the triumph on Mount Acidale, for the recreative impulse is significantly different from the moral or plaintive. Its object is not social improvement or a woman, but the activity of poetry itself, the play of the mind simply for its own sake—"the mind's delight in itself, in its power of excess and fantasy, in its ability to play the game of freedom, even freedom from law and the moral order."[26] The treasures of the muses may supplant the objects sought by savages, lovers, and heroes; found nowhere in nature, they must be created and objectified by the human spirit before they can exist over against the soul, as pleasures to be pursued. The recreative interest is not in the originals which poetry imitates but in the models and model-making power through which originals are explored.

If Pastorella and her circle are a more refined form of Serena and the cannibals; if the object of desire is heightened and enhanced by inhibition, by withdrawal to more symbolic forms of action; then the second image is still not simply a revised version of the first. The two are also parallel: the savage ring is the nursery of the first nature, the starting-point of culture as a whole; the pastoral ring is the nursery of the second nature, the deliberately reduced and purely artificial landscape of *topoi,* images, rhetorical figures, and phonetic structures which are the raw material of poetry. These first attract the poet simply as ornaments and jewels, or, to use a common Renaissance image, flowers.[27]

By reproducing the *Calender* world in all its flatness Spenser justifies the recreative delight in artifice. Artifice, as we understand the term when thinking of literary conventions, and as Renaissance thinkers certainly understood it—artifice displays the shaping hand of spirit and guarantees that meaning lurks beneath the surface of the form. As the Neoplatonist term *hieroglyph* suggests, a symbolic object must indicate, by various simplifications, its symbolic nature if the reader is to look beyond it; to make the rustic actual, as Spenser had done in the moral eclogues, is to dissipate its artificiality.[28] The conventional artifice may be nothing more than a sign, but it is the necessary blueprint or flat form on which the meaning is ultimately raised.

Thus, in the ninth canto, we return to the blueprint world,

the polyglot landscape of borrowed conventions which Spenser
had assembled in *The Shepheardes Calender*. We come upon
this place through a magical, a kind of Proustian, transforma-
tion: the blatant beast disappears and we are led with Calidore
out of chivalric Faerie, back in time to Spenser's early poetry.
All the space between vanishes—five books of Faerie, eight cantos
of Book VI, the arduous questing, plaintive or moral, which led
to this moment. The fullness of vision, the triumph of imagination, is suddenly sprung from the conventional platform as the
description of Pastorella reappears in its refined form: on top of
the mountain where "Venus, when she did dispose / Her selfe
to pleasaunce, used to resort / . . . and therein to repose / And
rest her self" (x.9) Calidore sees

> An hundred naked maidens lilly white,
> All raunged in a ring, and dauncing in delight.

> All they without were raunged in a ring,
>   And daunced round; but in the midst of them
>   Three other Ladies did both daunce and sing,
>   The whilest the rest them round about did hemme,
>   And like a girlond did in compasse stemme:
>   And in the middest of those same three, was placed
>   Another Damzell, as a precious gemme,
>   Amidst a ring most richly well enchaced,
> That with her goodly presence all the rest much graced.

> Looke how the Crowne, which Ariadne wore
>   Upon her yvory forehead that same day,
>   That Theseus her unto his bridale bore,
>   When the bold Centaures made that bloudy fray,

With the fierce Lapithes, which did them dismay;
Being now placed in the firmament,
Through the bright heaven doth her beames display,
And is unto the starres an ornament,
Which round about her move in order excellent.

Such was the beauty of this goodly band,
Whose sundry parts were here too long to tell:
But she that in the midst of them did stand,
Seem'd all the rest in beauty to excell,
Crownd with a rosie girlond, that right well
Did her beseeme. And ever, as the crew
About her daunst, sweet flowres, that far did smell,
And fragrant odours they uppon her threw;
But most of all, those three did her with gifts endew.

Those were the Graces, daughters of delight,
Handmaides of Venus, which are wont to haunt
Uppon this hill, and daunce there day and night:
Those three to men all gifts of grace do graunt,
And all, that Venus in her selfe doth vaunt,
Is borrowed of them. But that faire one,
That in the midst was placed paravaunt,
Was she to whom that shepheard pypt alone,
That made him pipe so merrily, as never none.

(x.11–15)

Then comes a sudden flashback to the simple original of this
vision, and an allusion to the plaintive experience, the frustration, which led to the sublime triumph and is included as part
of it:

> She was to weete that jolly Shepheards lasse,
>> Which piped there unto that merry rout,
>> That jolly shepheard, which there piped, was
>> Poore Colin Clout (who knowes not Colin Clout?)
>> He pypt apace, whilest they him daunst about.
>> Pype jolly shepheard, pype thou now apace
>> Unto thy love, that made thee low to lout:
>> Thy love is present there with thee in place,
> Thy love is there advaunst to be another Grace.
>
> (x.16)

Finally Colin, after revealing the genesis and emblematic significance of the Graces, describes the radiant center, the heart of
light into which Rosalind has been transfigured:

> But that fourth Mayd, which there amidst them traced,
> Who can aread, what creature mote she bee,
> Whether a creature, or a goddessse graced
> With heavenly gifts from heven first enraced?
> But what so sure she was, she worthy was,
> To be the fourth with those three other placed:
> Yet was she certes but a countrey lasse,
> Yet she all other countrey lasses farre did passe.
>
> So farre as doth the daughter of the day,
> All other lesser lights in light excell,
> So farre doth she in beautyfull array,
> Above all other lasses beare the bell,
> Ne lesse in virtue that beseemes her well,
> Doth she exceede the rest of all her race,
> For which the Graces that here wont to dwell,

Have for more honor brought her to this place,
And graced her so much to be another Grace.

Another Grace she well deserves to be,
   In whom so many Graces gathered are,
   Excelling much the meane of her degree,
   Divine resemblaunce, beauty soveraine rare,
   Firme Chastity, that spight ne blemish dare;
   All which she with such courtesie doth grace,
   That all her peres cannot with her compare,
   But quite are dimmed, when she is in place.
She made me often pipe and now to pipe apace.

Sunne of the world, great glory of the sky,
   That all the earth doest lighten with thy rayes,
   Great Gloriana, greatest Majesty,
   Pardon thy shepheard, mongst so many layes,
   As he hath sung of thee in all his dayes,
   To make one minime of thy poore handmayd,
   And underneath thy feete to place her prayse,
   That when thy glory shall be farre displayd
To future age of her this mention may be made.

                                          (x.25–28)

Here two voices merge in one, Colin as he speaks, Spenser as he
writes, the man momentarily transformed into the pure poetic
voice, the recreative voice re-created, the past leaping to new life
in the present. It is the moment of second sight in which the poet
returns to his early fragments of insight, inspiration, or mere
sportive pleasure and revises them, *sees* them for the first time.
The past and present are juxtaposed as promise and fulfillment

in a single poetic form, and the oscillation between them is sustained by the fact that Spenser keeps unworked pastoral elements in the later vision.

In this great passage there is not only the circling of thought which unites the parts of time, but the circling of words in rhythmic repetition, echoing and reechoing, as they imitate the movement of the figures around a center beyond the reach of language; and at the same time the rising and cresting of vision as it moves from the dale to Ariadne's crown, then returns to Colin, Rosalind, and Calidore only to ascend once more, in Colin's explication, to the Sun of the world. Perhaps in that first lyric outcry of discovery, when the entire episode is momentarily grasped in the image of Ariadne's crown, we may best see the luminous compression of Spenser's thought.[29] The crown of a mortal placed high in the visible heavens is a ring round which the stars move in order excellent, and this is compared to the dance of the three Graces circled by the hundred auxiliary graces. The comparison unites the heavenly and imaginary dances, the physical and mental orders, the actual zodiac and the zodiac of the poet's wit.

But the subject of the simile is the imaginary rather than the actual cosmos, the dance rather than the constellation. Even in the comparison, the constellation appears as the result and symbol of a human experience; its meaning is referred not to its divine creator but to the manmade myth. As the crown gives way to the "rosie girlond" of the central figure, it embellishes the pastoral dance which, while remaining pastoral, resonates with the full amplitude of the cosmic harmony. The rosy garland of the *Shepheardes Calender* displays its glory throughout the universe

visibly ordered now—after long pain—by the poet's "fayning."
And in this movement it is not simply the described figures but
the vision itself which seems stanza by stanza to shift and re-
volve, expand and contract, unfolding as if the poet does not
know what he thinks till he sees what he says. The landscape
displays a mind negatively capable, an indeterminate and creative collaboration between the epic poet and his pastoral persona.

Thus our first view is of a place visibly emerging from, or involved with, certain typical Spenserian themes:

> It was an hill plaste in an open plaine,
>   That round about was bordered with a wood
>   Of matchlesse hight, that seem'd th' earth to disdaine,
>   In which all trees of honour stately stood,
>   And did all winter as in sommer bud,
>   Spreadding pavilions for the birds to bowre,
>   Which in their lower braunches sung aloud;
>   And in their tops the soring hauke did towre,
> Sitting like King of fowles in majesty and powre.
>
> And at the foote thereof, a gentle flud
>   His silver waves did softly tumble downe,
>   Unmard with ragged mosse or filthy mud,
>   Ne mote wylde beastes, ne mote the ruder clowne
>   Thereto approach, ne filth mote therein drowne:
>   But Nymphes and Faeries by the bancks did sit,
>   In the woods shade, which did the waters crowne,
>   Keeping all noysome things away from it,
> And to the waters fall tuning their accents fit.   (x.6–7)

This is the second nature spun by human desire and art; the actual and ugly are excluded by fiat as the choice bits once sampled in the Muses' Elizium are collected in a new setting, deep within the mind; the aristocratic disdain is that of the second nature for the first. The essence of this place is that it is totally meaningful, human intention projected as image: "And on the top thereof a spacious plaine / Did spred it selfe, to serve to all delight" (x.8). The place was called Acidale *because* it seemed "to overlooke the lowly vale" of early pastoral, also because the prospect is far from care and serves to all delight.

But Acidale is also the Graces' fountain and turns the mind toward a mythic possibility,

> They say that Venus, when she did dispose
> Her selfe to pleasaunce, used to resort
> Unto this place, and therein to repose
> And rest her selfe, as in a gladsome port,
> Or with the Graces there to play and sport. . . .
>
> (x.9)

The parallel suggests a further meaning for Spenser's private place: the Queen of Beauty, whose "goodly formes and faire aspects" (III.vi.12) make her the Mother of Love, comes here not to exercise her creative powers but simply to delight in them. It is a second holiday, wayward yet rhythmic, amid the embodied Ideas produced by the mind's "tedious travell." The imagination looks at what it has made, sees that it is very good, and hopes to attract something more real than itself, the universal symbol of that God which is the source of its energy. The Graces

are not yet here and now, since the convergence is put off by
the phrase "they say." The landscape is first solidified into something concrete and sensuous so that the recreative delight is
seen and heard and felt, but does not yet release its new meaning. Calidore hears "the merry sound" of Colin's pipe and "many
feete fast thumping th' hollow ground" (x.10), and then he sees
the "hundred naked maidens lilly white." This pastoral image
is immediately expanded and etherealized—the Ariadne comparison looks like a sudden inspiration, since it is an apostrophe
in the present tense—and just as quickly contracted to the "rosie
girlond." The Graces now appear in person, the vision is further
contracted in the second apostrophe to Colin, after which it
vanishes. Even without Calidore's intrusion, the descriptive
rhythm anticipates this outcome, and one feels that however long
Spenser's hidden recreative voice has invoked the vision it is
unfolded only now, in the brevity of the present fulfillment.

The episode as a whole circles through three familiar emphases:
First, the vision of delight, where the earliest recreation becomes
the latest re-creation. Second, the plaintive moment in which the
vision is interrupted and Colin again breaks his pipe. Third, the
moral emphasis when Colin converts the vision into an emblem.
Here, he has replaced E.K.; this would have been unthinkable
in the *Calender,* where the amplitude of life and meaning was
precisely what that first world of conventions excluded. But now
Colin catches up the recreative and plaintive moments into the
moral. Love, poetry, and morality converge—"Divine resemblaunce, beauty soveraine rare, / Firme Chastity." All become
eros, the latest gift and the earliest source. For it was *eros* that
led him years ago to fall in love, and moved him to confront the

fox and ape, and above all impelled him to play with words, to become a poet long before he could know *why* he was so inclined —*eros* was the true source of even that mindless joy. What began in the realm of the Muses ends in the realm of the Graces. One thinks especially of the *April* eclogue, the meaning of whose forms remained inert in the gloss taken from dictionaries and handbooks. But one is also reminded of the country lass who denied her love, and one realizes that when the poet's amorous insight finally yields its refined Acidalian form, the handmaids of Venus have in effect become muses.

Colin's account does more than explain the vanished dance: it imports into Spenser's Acidale the rich iconographic tradition of Venus and the Graces elaborated by the human mind in its long cultural dialectic.[30] He begins, again with the widest perspective: the Graces are daughters of "sky-ruling Jove" and Eurynome, "The Oceans daughter" (x.22); effects of cosmic force and fertility, justice and generosity, but in Spenser's variation effects produced only on Acidale in a moment of repose and gratuitous delight. The catalogue of their qualities leads to a new image of the Graces:

> two of them still froward seem'd to bee,
> But one still towards shew'd her selfe afore;
> That good should from us goe, then come in greater store.
>
> (x.24)

The dance is a diaphanous shimmer of meaning and image, turning and interacting, each modifying the other. The Graces are unfolded from Venus in their ancient and familiar poses, advance concretely before us, display their meanings, then fade into qualities as they are infolded by Colin's beloved: "Another Grace she well deserves to be, / In whom so many Graces gathered are." For a moment the beloved is poised alone in visionary splendor; in the next moment she recedes to make room for Gloriana though, with the words "Sunne of the world," the two Ideas make brief contact. The lyric muse reveals her affinity to the epic muse and the vision gives way to the narrative of Book vi.

In that momentary poise, however, and in the circling dance, the vision resonates with harmonious echoes. We may recall the revelation on the mountain top in Book i, and the other in the Gardens of Adonis; the hundred virgins in the temple of Venus; the image of Amoret surrounded by her garland of virtues. The vision is the solution and resolution of all the problems, all the motifs, suggested in earlier parts of the book: the aristocracy and foundling motifs; the nursery, withdrawal and retirement motifs; the motifs of love, of holiday and diversion, of being caught off guard, turning inward—all these, along with the previous circles, are now revealed as symbols and dim prefigurations of Acidale. And at the center of the ring of graces is no single creature but a richly complicated knot of all the figures the poet has ever meditated on—Rosalind, Elizabeth, Amoret, Belphoebe, Florimell, Britomart, Venus, Psyche—"Who can aread, what creature mote she bee"? Unlike Pastorella, she has no name, is beyond names; though she has been in part generated from the fictional domain of names and images in the dance of meanings, she has, so to speak, been sprung from this domain, having been "enchaced" by his thought distilled from so much "tedious travell." He has not ever taken his eye off that first form, the simple country lass, but whoever she is in herself no longer matters. The form has been refined until the beloved has become love, the hieroglyph of *eros*—not an *other,* but a vision or symbol or concept of whatever it is that draws us toward the other.[31]

In its context and in its form, the vision enacts the Neoplatonic idea that the soul is a foundling, an aristocrat long ignorant of its true source. It confuses its principle with primitive beginnings, with something temporally prior and externally simpler, like savagery or rusticity. The true beginning and principle is neither in time nor in space but always vivid at the center, deep within the mind. Only by turning inward, by self-creation, by tirelessly seeking and wooing and invoking the muses, or *eros,* or what lies behind them all—only thus do we regain our long-lost heritage. By some process akin to anamnesis we withdraw, we retire, we return to the nursery, we close the circle of beginnings and endings, we come finally to that first Idea, that pure grace which has always moved us. And our point of contact with the real is the moving geometric form, the dynamism of thought itself. What is felt as divine is not the vision itself so much as the sense of having been given—the sense of a richness and variety, a copious world of forms and meanings which the mind produces *as if* by its own reflex activity, but really by the grace of God. The divine, the real, are now sought for only in their transfigured forms, and they are found not in the transfiguration but in the activity, the process of transfiguring. So the *Faerie Queene* swings on its great axis from the objective reality of Dante's universe, to which Book 1 is closest, toward the symbolic form of *Paradise Lost.*

It is important to take into account the presence of Rosalind as a simple country lass and poor handmaid of Gloriana, if one is to do justice to the realistic basis of Spenser's vision. The triumph of imagination is partly measured by the extent to which it has converted frustration, brute fact, the world of first sight and first nature, into a symbolic intuition of the real; the presence of the country lass and the early pastoral testifies to this triumph. But the triumph is also measured by acceptance of what the mind cannot transform, by the awareness of limit which Clarion must learn the hard way. The complete self-sufficiency of the second nature, the total inward mastery of experience—this is no triumph at all, only delusion, if it takes itself seriously. For then it would have nothing to do with the poet *now,* a man still faced by life, fortune, malice, Providence. Thus poetry, having triumphed, must dissolve its triumph again and again to show that it is still engaged in the ongoing process of life where experience is not yet ordered. On Mount Acidale, when the play of mind realizes its vision, the poet dissolves it and moves on. In vision the mind objectifies its desires and intuitions so that it can see and respond; Colin's explanation is the response of the mind to the figure it has made and which it accepts as given. But just as the explanation acknowledges the persistence of the country lass, so the poem returns to the blatant beast and to its own dissolution. Spenser's poetic style is generated from the awareness that the poetic universe must be circumscribed as artifice and play; yet within the circumscribed place the poet must adumbrate the raw, the meaningless, so that we see it in the poem but outside the poetry. The secret discipline of imagination is a double burden, discordant and harmonious: first, its delight in the power and freedom of art; second, the controlled surrender whereby it acknowledges the limits of artifice. For Spenser, who is among the true poets, the vision must be bounded and shaped by the sense that it is not reality; and it must yield to reality at last.

Mutabilitie and the Cycle of the Months

> . . . we all beholde as in a mirrour the glorie of the Lord with un-
> veiled face, and are changed into the same image, from glorie to
> glorie, as by the Spirit of the Lord   (II Cor. 3.18).

CRITICS OF THE Mutabilitie Cantos have sometimes felt that, although Nature silences Mutabilitie, her verdict comes from Spenser's heart rather than his head. The Cantos express his despair,
confronted by the universal rule of change,

> Which makes me loath this state of life so tickle,
> And loue of things so vaine to cast away.[1]

But these lines come at the end of the Mutabilitie Cantos, and if
we take them as expressing the mood and meaning of the entire
poem, there is danger we will read it backwards. The pessimistic
interpretation involves two other mistakes, it seems to me. The
first of these is the tacit assumption that constancy means changelessness, and that all change therefore is inconstancy. This is a
conceptual error. The second error is structural, and consists in
ignoring the symbolic center of the Cantos, the pageant of the
months and seasons. This pageant is introduced by Mutabilitie
as final proof of her claims, and here, if anywhere, the evidence
for Nature's verdict will be found.

Let us look at the conceptual problem first. What does Spenser mean by mutability and constancy? C. S. Lewis, I think, goes too far in equating Mutabilitie with sin and corruption.[2] The Titanesse is blamed for death and old age and the fall of man, but she also causes changes as innocent as the random movements of fish, of wind and water, and as desirable as spring or growing up. She is, then, simply what Spenser calls her in his proems, "Change" or "Alteration." As child of Titan and Earth and granddaughter of Chaos, she is allied on the mother's side with inchoate matter, and on the father's with rebellious pride, for Spenser associates the Titans with the giants who revolted against Jove. But we notice that Mutabilitie's sisters, who share this sinister parentage, have received great power and high authority from Jove. Hecate and Bellona—or Fortune and War—work as parts of the divine plan administered by Jove, though their working may seem dark and inexplicable to human eyes. A similar function is open to Mutabilitie. But she refuses to "seeke by grace and goodnesse to obtaine / That place from which by folly *Titan* fell." Mutabilitie is not sin, but it is sin which sends her in revolt against the gods, repeating the error of her father, the primal rebel. Yet this rebellious creature is described as beautiful—

> Beeing of stature tall as any there
> Of all the Gods, and beautifull of face. . . .

This beauty stays the Thunderbearer's hand, "Such sway doth beauty euen in Heauen beare," and Spenser's insistence on the beauty of change underlies all the intellectual complexities of the Cantos.

Mutabilitie claims the sovereignty of heaven and earth both *de jure* and *de facto,* in Canto 6 by right of lineage, in Canto 7 as an accomplished fact. Jove, she complains, has superseded the older line of Titan, and thus we have the delightful spectacle of Mutabilitie indicting mutability and Change railing against change. But primacy in metaphysics does not depend on priority in time. Though chaos precedes order, it has, as a principle, no greater reality or right. Thus Spenser makes Hate the elder brother of Love:

> Yet was the younger stronger in his state
> Then th' elder, and him maystred still in all debate.

> (IV.x.32.8–9)

Jove does not justify his rule by temporal priority but by conquest and "eternall doome of Fates decree." In other words, order has "maystred" chaos, and this change, decreed even before time, represents the will of Providence. In this instance, there is meaning in mutability.

This is the very point which Mutabilitie challenges in Canto 7. She claims to rule the world, and she easily proves that all things change. No one disputes that. But the change she pictures is a denial of purpose and law. Change is a law unto itself—indeed, the only law governing the phenomenal world. All things, including man, change simply for the love of changing, for "all that moueth, doth mutation loue." Now the universe envisaged by Spenser's contemporaries is indeed a world in motion, and it is love which moves this world—but not the love of moving. The Elizabethan concept of motion is philosophic and not scientific, explaining movement by its goal rather than its source: it is the difference between a physics of push and a metaphysics of pull. All things, Richard Hooker explains, have an "appetite or desire" for perfection, and thus they move and change towards an end, the perfection peculiar to their natures.[3] Since God, the first mover, is absolute perfection, they seek to participate in Him as far as their natures permit. Law is not opposed to change, but regulates its mode and force. Love gives change direction; law gives it settled course. Nature's choice, then, is not between changelessness and change, but between the aimlessness of change for its own sake, and the constancy of movement directed by love and law towards a perfect goal. Nature gives her verdict without hesitation: things are not changed from their first estate

> But by their change their being doe dilate:
> And turning to themselues at length againe,
> Doe worke their owne perfection so by fate:
> Then ouer them Change doth not rule and raigne;
> But they raigne ouer change, and doe their states maintaine.

In other words, all things conquer change by achieving a perfection implicit in their origin; they finally become what they were first created to be. Since God is the source and end of this movement, its efficient and its final cause, the movement is a circle. For creatures lacking reason, this is a natural process; their cycles are controlled by destiny. But since man used his freedom to violate the law of his nature, he must now seek his end by a "way which is supernaturall,"[4] the way of grace opened to him in the Incarnation. He too moves in a circle, working to restore in himself the original righteousness of Adam, but now in the more perfect image of Christ. The fall has made this a cycle of labors: but if man is constant to the law of his supernatural way, he too can make his circle just and end where he began. And this

suggests the irony which Spenser intends in presenting the cycle
of the months and their labors as proof of the aimlessness of
change.

What of Nature and Jove, the other major figures in the
Cantos? Nature is here, I think, the Wisdom or Sapience which,
in the "Hymne of Heauenly Beautie," rules all things so that they
"do in state remaine, / As their great Maker did at first ordaine." [5]
Nature, like Wisdom in Apocrypha, is more beautiful than the
sun: her face cannot be seen "but like an image in a glass." [6]
In his "Hymne," Spenser explains that we cannot endure the
direct brightness of God's face, but we can behold its image in
the looking-glass of his created works. Then by degrees of contemplation we rise to look upon the "celestiall face" of Sapience.[7]
In the same way, the creatures at Arlo Hill, not yet ready to look
on Nature's face unveiled, may yet behold the works of Wisdom
in the labors of the months—like an image in a glass. Wisdom,
the ordering power which creates and sustains the universe, appears to them in the guise of Nature. And the name of the judge
defines the area in dispute. Mutabilitie claims to rule both nature
and man, and we notice that although the months are human
beings, they are workers in the fields and vineyards, who labor to
bring the fruits of earth to their perfection. The dispute is over
man in nature, and Spenser refuses to dissociate the way of grace
by which man attains salvation from the natural movement of
the rest of creation. Both together constitute the "nature" Mutabilitie claims to rule, and her claim is therefore judged by the
power Spenser calls the "God of Nature." It could be argued that
the meaning of the Cantos would be different if Spenser named
his umpire Jove, or Grace, or simply God.

Wisdom is that stability of the divine thought which orders all change and generation. As referred to God, this stable order is called Providence; as referred to his creatures and acting in time, it is called Destiny. This distinction, familiar from Boethius to Richard Hooker, is lucidly explained by Justus Lipsius in his *Two Bookes of Constancie*. Destiny operates within the created order: it is the *"immooueble decree of Prouidence inherent in things mooueable."* But Destiny represents only one aspect of Necessity. The other is a "naturall propertie to all things created, to fall into mutabilitie and alteration." [8] Thus Lipsius helps us understand the functions of Spenser's principal characters. Nature corresponds to Providence, the divine Wisdom that decrees; Jove and the planets represent Destiny, which executes these decrees in the temporal world; while Mutabilitie is that tendency to change inherent in all created things, which is the other aspect of Necessity. Langius, the instructor of Lipsius in the dialogue, runs through all the evidence of change: like Mutabilitie herself, he shows that the stars have varied their fashion and their course; that the air, the waters and earth are altered; that there is war among the elements; that every man passes through youth and strength to old age and death. Lift up your eyes, he urges Lipsius: behold the alterations in all human affairs and "let this wheel of changeable things run round, so long as this round world re-mayneth." Dismayed by the vanity of human life, Lipsius breaks into tears: What are these things for which we toil? he cries. *"Man is a shadowe and a dreame."* But Langius replies: "Imprint CONSTANCIE in thy mind amid this casuall and inconstant variablenesse of all things. I call it inconstant in respect of our vnderstanding and judgment: for that if thou looke vnto God and his prouidence, all things succeed in a steddy and immoueable order." The necessity of change, which seems the evidence of disorder and decay, actually testifies to this immovable order. "Thinkest thou that CHAVNCE or FORTVNE beareth any sway in this excellent frame of the world? . . . I wot well thou thinkest not so, nor any man els that hath either wisdom or wit in his head." The voice of nature itself, wheresoever we turn our eyes or minds, cries out that there is an eternal spirit we call God "which ruleth, guideth and gouerneth the rolling Spheares of heauen, the manifolde courses of the Stars and Planets, the successiu alterations of the Elements, finally, al things whatsoeuer in heauen and earth." [9] Thus Lipsius shows how the whole of Mutabilitie's argument for change fits into a larger argument for constancy. It would seem that Spenser's solution comes from his head as well as his heart.

This hierarchy of powers—Nature, Jove, and Mutabilitie—suggests a triple interpretation of constancy as a virtue of the intellect, the affections, and the will. All constancy ultimately depends on the stability of the divine understanding, working by a law which Hooker tells us can "haue no shew or cullor of mutabilitie." [10] Constancy, then, is first of all an intellectual virtue, finding stability in contemplation of the wisdom of Providence, represented here by Nature. Secondly, constancy in relation to the passions is steadfast fortitude, whose patient endurance remains unmoved by Mutabilitie and her wheel of change. Thirdly, as a virtue of the active will, it is perseverance, the unswerving pursuit of the course of Destiny, here figured by Jove and the other planets. This is virtue in motion, and, like natural law, it attains stability in its unchanging direction and its changeless end. As Nicholas Breton writes in his "Praise of Constancie,"

> It set the course of Wisedomes cariage,
> And neuer further then affection went:
> It is the state of all perfections stay,
> And Times all euerlasting holy day.[11]

I should now like to turn from the conceptual problem to more concrete problems of tone and structure. The obvious fact about the tone of the Cantos is its variety. Spenser's mimic world is inclusive and hospitable. His Grecian myth triumphantly assimilates its Irish setting: the imagined reality finds room for both the crystal pillars of Diana's palace and the salmon swimming in the Shure. Yet this variety is without confusion. The entire natural creation gathers at Arlo Hill: it is Nature's sergeant, Order, who finds each creature his due place in his degree. Spenser's delight in the fertile variety of things, and his deep confidence in the order which underlies variety, account for the varied texture of the Cantos and the unusual solidity of the objects they contain. The tone, as C. S. Lewis points out, is infinitely flexible: it rises to Olympian councils and descends without faltering to the rustic humors of foolish god Faunus.[12] And if it is flexible, it is firm: the sure and gracious movement of the verse seems to preclude the possibility of aimlessness in the poet's creation and in the greater creation which the poet imitates.

A definite purpose directs these changes of tone. We noticed that Spenser makes Mutabilitie responsible both for degeneration and decay and also for changes which are quite harmless and innocent. He does not distinguish between the ideas that "all things change" and that "all things change for the worse." This deliberate ambiguity permits him to alter his tone subtly but definitely in the course of the Cantos. He states the darkest implications of Mutabilitie at the very beginning: here she is associated with Adam's fall, Satan's rebellion, and the gradual decay of the world. But in Canto 7, when Mutabilitie presents her own case, she is associated with morally neutral mutations of creatures, elements, and times. This transition from "unnatural" to natural change alters our conception of change itself from our fallen predicament to our natural condition, and prepares us for the pageant of months, in which change becomes almost our opportunity.

The structure of Cantos 6 and 7 is markedly symmetrical. In each, an abstract debate is followed by a more concrete pictorial episode, the interlude of Faunus and Molanna, and the pageant of the times. Both episodes are relevant and functional. The buffoonery of the pastoral interlude is a parody of Mutabilitie's revolt. Thus in both halves of the sixth canto, a demigod assaults Diana. This is appropriate, for Diana is an emblem of constant inconstancy. Below the moon all things change; above it circle the unchanging heavens; the lunar sphere is the border between mutability and the immutable. The moon, which monthly changes in its circled orb, is a type of all inconstancy, "So that *as changefull as the Moone* men vse to say," and Spenser notes that Cynthia "neuer still did stand." Her very identity is triple in heaven, on earth, and in the underworld, and her changes are directly responsible for the changing months of the next Canto. On the other hand, as goddess of chastity, Diana is a type of constancy. Cynthia is a name for the Virgin Queen, whose motto was *Semper eadem,* always the same.[13] The parallel invasions of Canto 6 are directed against Diana in her double role: Mutabilitie attacks the divine power who is most changeable, while Faunus attempts the type of virgin constancy.

Faunus, half god, half goat, is closely related to Pan, whose dual nature was allegorized as the heavens and earth which make up the universe. His goatish legs, says Abraham Fraunce, betoken the crooked course of things under the moon, for these observe no immutable order. Pan pursues the spotless virgin Syrinx because universal nature desires a "celestiall and perpetuall constancy in these inferior bodies." [14] So we can see how the story of Faunus' lust for the goddess of chaste constancy fits into a debate on mutability. But plot and subplot are closely modeled on other classical myths. Mutabilitie's invasion of the skies recalls Phaeton, who also invaded heaven to demand his birthright, while Faunus recalls Actaeon, who was likewise hunted as a deer after he saw Diana bathing. Spenser uses these myths, I think, to hint at the primary myth of the fall. Phaeton is a type of pride, and Mutabilitie's ambitious revolt suggests the intellectual pride which made man aspire to be as God. Faunus represents the other aspect of the fall, the element of animal concupiscence: Actaeon torn by his hounds is man devoured by his animal passions. Mutabilitie's hybris is the stuff of tragedy, but the follies of the flesh are theme for comedy, so Spenser abates the sternness of his style in relating them. But the fall is essential to an account of mutability, and very lightly, very allusively, Spenser reminds us of its reality. Faunus tempts Molanna with "Queene-apples, and red Cherries from the tree"—the analogies with the Eden story are obvious enough. Faunus, like Satan, is punished in animal guise, while

Molanna, like Eve, is sentenced to death for her inconstancy. But
the episode is allusive and resists strict allegory. If Faunus' role
as tempter recalls Satan, his subservience to appetite suggests
Adam, as does his hunger for forbidden knowledge. The Actaeon
story, according to Fraunce, teaches that "we ought not to be ouer
curious and inquisitiue in spying and prying into those matters,
which be aboue our reache." [15] Both Mutabilitie and Faunus break
in upon assemblies of the gods, and finally Nature must appear,
like Diana, without a veil to satisfy the Titanesse. But Diana,
when she is spied upon, abandons Arlo Hill, a motif recalling the
departure of Astraea at the end of the first golden age. Thus
abandoned by its deity, the paradise of Arlo Hill falls prey to
wolves and thieves.[16] The same wolves lurk in the pastoral landscape of *Lycidas,* and we have not done with them yet, for we
are all "in-dwellers" of that fallen country, and Spenser's myth,
as he himself declares, is "too-too true." But at the beginning of
the seventh canto, we see the coming of a divinity greater than
Diana for a final judgment, and now Arlo is transfigured like
Mount Thabor in a second golden age. What seemed a triumph
of mutability turns out to be a cycle, ending in greater perfection
than before: the episode repeats the meaning of the whole.

Faunus also marks a new stage in our understanding of nature,
for nature, like mutability, is a concept which changes and develops in the poem. As we first see it, the fair frame of the universe
is so perverted that "all this world is woxen daily worse." This
state of decay and disorder seems inimical to Diana and the constancy she represents. Faunus, whose form reflects a doubleness
in nature, is one step closer to order. Certainly he is anything but
hostile to Diana, but he represents an unshaped world of impulse

and appetite, incapable of either love or law. The divine beauty
which lures him produces neither reverence nor real desire—only
an inchoate excitement which breaks out in laughter. Contrast
the response of the created world to Nature herself in Canto 7.
At her bright coming the earth puts forth voluntary flowers, and
all creatures are ranged in order by her decree. The natural world
is now seen as orderly and fertile, though fertility remains dominant. Even old Father Mole has changed his grey attire to green,
"As if the loue of some new Nymph late seene, / Had in him
kindled youthfull fresh desire." At this level of barely sentient
life, response to the divine does not distinguish between worship
and desire, goddess and nymph. But the joy of the old mountain
and the flowering earth is instinct with reverence: the divine and
the natural are in harmony as once before on Haemus hill at the
marriage of Peleus and Thetis, the union of god and man, where
Phoebus sang the "spousall hymne full cleere." We hardly need
the *Ovide moralisé en prose* to identify that marriage feast with
the *paradis terrestre* in which man lived before the apple thrown
by Discord, that *diable d'enfer,* began our woe.[17] And it is against
this background of natural harmony, of paradise regained, that
Mutabilitie introduces the conflict of the elements as evidence of
change. Actually it is, both traditionally and elsewhere in Spenser,
an argument for concord and stability, and we begin to suspect
that Mutabilitie is the victim of a vast dramatic irony.

   This is, in fact, the case; but Spenser is a poet, not a philosopher:
he gives us his essential realities in images, not arguments. As the
pageant of the months bursts upon us, logic gives way to picture.
It is easy for us to lose the argument in the profusion of sensuous
imagery, but pictures spoke for the Elizabethans. They were ac-

customed to interpret such rich disguisings, where more is meant
than meets the eye. The entrance of the months and seasons resembles the climax of a masque: we have had the allegorical *débat*
and the comic antimasque: now in glorious procession the
masquers march before us. The Jonsonian masque is, of course,
a later development; but, like Jonson, Spenser uses the revelation
of his "masquers" to mark the turning point, the defeat of the
forces of disorder, the establishment of harmony in color, music,
and motion. Spenser feels no need to interpret his pageant: the
splendor of the vision, its order and its perfect rightness, should
suffice.

But the modern reader needs to be reminded that Spenser's
imagery belongs to a very old iconographical tradition. For cen-
turies the months and their labors appeared over and over again
in calendars and books of hours, above the portals of cathedrals,
in handbooks and encyclopedias, signifying that the divisions of
time—winter and summer, seedtime and harvest, days and years—
are part of the divine plan, and that by labor man works out his
own place in it. The medieval man who paused to contemplate
the great stone calendar over a church door found various meanings there, according to Emile Mâle—and all of them apply to
Spenser's calendar. The laborer recognized his own unceasing
round of work, but the statue of the Savior looking down on
these things of earth reminded him that he did not work without hope. The churchman, knowing that each month in the
church calendar marks some event in the life of Christ or some
great saint, saw them as a sequence of heroic acts: to him the
year seemed like a garland of the virtues. The mystic saw in time
the shadow of eternity and the year itself as a figure of Christ.[18]

No doubt sheer repetition often obscured this complex of meanings and the labors of the months were reproduced as ornaments or mere conventions. Indeed, the modern reader is likely to assume either that such highly conventional figures can have no special meaning in Spenser's poem or that Spenser was simply repeating some explicit and generally accepted symbolism. Neither assumption is correct. It was not difficult for a fourteenth-century allegorist like Pierre Bersuire to translate the months, complete with etymologies, labors, and zodiacal signs, into elaborate symbols of twelve vices and virtues. The just man, perfected in all these virtues, is like the tree of life in Revelation which bears twelve manner of fruit and yields her fruit each month.[19] Bersuire shows how far the symbolic interpretation of these stereotyped figures could be carried. But his systematic and detailed medieval allegories differ from Spenser's both in method and result. Spenser aims neither to repeat nor to invent. He is a traditional poet in a sense we have almost forgotten: he strives to penetrate and revive the central meaning in these images, so profoundly suggestive and so old, to recreate this meaning for a specific poetic purpose. The result is a genuine act of creative imagination, which can be understood only in the double perspective of a long history and an immediate poetic context. And the details of this poetic context require careful scrutiny.

At first glance Spenser's seasons seem to favor Mutabilitie. Rabanus Maurus tells us that spring represents the resurrection and renewal of life. Summer symbolizes the warmth of charity and prefigures the joys of the blest. Autumn, season of harvest and grape-gathering, refers to the Last Judgment, and winter signifies tribulation and the end of mortal life.[20] But these mean-

ings are not active here—at least not yet. Spenser's Ovidian images
of the seasons are brilliant but rather blank. Like the ages of man
which represent them, the seasons seem to move in cycles without
a goal: youth, maturity, decay, followed by the spring of another
generation, another year. But there is regularity here: Spring
doesn't follow Summer, nor Autumn Spring. The seasons are
marshaled by Order, who is Nature's sergeant, and this order, this
regular and repeated sequence, scarcely supports the claims of
restless and uncertain change, self-fed and self-consumed.

Spenser begins his months with March. The choice, though
commonplace, is significant. After Julius Caesar reformed the
calendar, the secular year always began on January 1. This remained New Year's Day throughout the Middle Ages and the
Renaissance. But it was originally a pagan festival. The Church
remembered that the world was created in March, and that after
the Exodus, God had designated this month as the beginning of
months, the first of the year (Exodus 12.2). When dating from
Christmas and Easter proved impractical, the Church began the
year on March 25, or Lady Day. This was the date of the Annun-
ciation, the beginning of the Christian era, and therefore the
proper beginning for what came to be called the "Year of Incarnation" or the "Year of Grace." The year *ab incarnatione
Domini* thus coincided with the year *a passione Domini,* since that
event too was thought to have occurred on March 25. The cycle
was perfect. Though January continued to be the first month in
calendars and almanacs, all official documents in England followed the dating of the "Year of Grace" until the middle of the
eighteenth century.[21]

The Year of Grace offered several advantages to Spenser. Most obviously, it matched the sequence of his months with that of the seasons. It also allowed him to suggest religious implications which would be obscured in the cycle from January to January. He had used this cycle in *The Shepheardes Calender,* but the symbolism had to be explained by E.K. in bald prose:

> . . . we mayntaine a custome of coumpting the seasons from the moneth Ianuarye, vpon a more speciall cause, then the heathen Philosophers euer coulde conceiue, that is, for the incarnation of our mighty Sauiour and eternall redeemer the L. Christ, who as then renewing the state of the decayed world, and returning the compasse of expired yeres to theyr former date and first commencement, left to vs his heires a memoriall of his birth in the ende of the last yeere and beginning of the next . . . ("The generall argument of the whole booke").

This symbolism was inherent in the very structure of the Year of Incarnation. Finally, beginning with March allowed Spenser to harmonize nature and grace as he had already done in the figure of Nature herself.[22] This calendar synchronizes the life of Christ with the progress of the seasons, the cycle of grace with the cycle of nature, "renewing the state of the decayed world" in both a spiritual and a physical sense. The same Providence is at work in the cycle of natural time and in the progress of redemptive history.

As the months march past, we note that almost all of them are laborers. Most of them carry farming tools: so eager is Spenser

to make his point that July, who has cast away all his garments
for the heat, nevertheless wears a sickle beneath his belt. Even old
January's hands are numbed

> with holding all the day
> An hatchet keene, with which he felled wood,
> And from the trees did lop the needlesse spray. . . .

This work moves with the steady rhythm of the seasons, the
quickening and decay of all green things. We are watching man
in nature, but we notice that man uses nature for his human ends.
The burgeoning of spring is directed towards a harvest. And
when that harvest is in, it is time to begin planning for the coming year: February has with him

> His plough and harnesse fit to till the ground,
> And tooles to prune the trees, before the pride
> Of hasting Prime did make them burgein round . . .

Man's foresight imposes a direction on the cycle of the months.
Yet we are not made to feel that man is "above" nature or that
he violates its meaning. His purposes are immanent in the natural processes themselves, so that man's end and nature's seem
the same. December's feasting is what the harvest and its fruits
are for.

This suggests another point. The labor is not felt as a burden.
It is hard work, and November's brows "reek and steem" with
sweat. Even the player, "iolly *Iune,*" has with him his plough
irons, and "in his time, he wrought as well as playd." Yet we are
always conscious of the rewards of labor, and of a strong current
of joy and affirmation that bears the months along. This is the

joy of that strong generative power which impels the endless succession of seeds and sexes, the bull all garlanded with flowers and horned with golden studs, his sides wet with the waves "through which he waded for his loues delight." It is the joy of sheer abundance, of the harvest riches which fill December's "broad deepe boawle" and turn October's totty head with "ioyous oyle, whose gentle gust / Made him so frollick and so full of lust." It is the quick joy of life itself, which dances at the very sight of May:

> Lord! how all creatures laught, when her they spide,
> And leapt and daunc't as they had rauisht beene!

And there are hints of another kind of joy, which is harder to define, in the picture of August with his "garment all of gold downe to the ground" and in that Lady he leads by the hand. But even when joy is past, when January shivers in the cold, still there is work to do, and a reason and a will to do it.

Labor, we remember, is one of the punishments of Adam's sin, and his sons win their bread by the sweat of their brow. But these sowers and harvesters and grape gatherers recall the Biblical parables in which men labor for a different wage. According to Augustine, there are two kinds of work. "For it is on account of the love of this world that men labor in all their affairs: but do you labor in all good works, not for the love of this world, but for the eternal rest which God promises." [23] What of Spenser's laborers? Do they work for the world and for the world's bread? Or do they labor in all good works towards the endless rest when "no more *Change* shall be"?

The answer is to be found in five months, some having no labors of their own, which suggest the values that inspire and sanction the labors of the others. April clearly represents fertility: he is "full of lustyhed" and "wanton as a Kid" and he is mounted upon Europa's bull. In May fertility evolves into love: May is a lovely girl, borne on the shoulders of the Gemini and strewing flowers from her lap. To make sure we do not miss the point, Spenser adds a Cupid, fluttering about her, "all in greene."

The fertility of seedtime ripens into August, the month of harvest. He leads forth Virgo, "the which was cround / With eares of corne, and full her hand was found." Paradoxically, it is Virgo who brings fertility to consummation. She represents the temperance without which abundance grows to wilderness, the chastity without which love is an expense of spirit in a waste of shame. This is justice as principle of nature; the "righteous Virgin" is, of course, Astraea. The paradox is only apparent: the laws of proportion and restraint are for Spenser and Milton as natural as the generative power itself. And just as the fertility of April develops into human love in May, so the natural justice of August becomes human and social justice in September. He carries a pair of scales with which he measures out the harvest, "And equall gaue to each as Iustice duly scann'd." They are, of course, Astraea's scales, for "next her selfe her righteous ballance hanging bee" (v.i.11.9).

Thus in Spenser's calendar, April and May are balanced by August and September: seedtime and harvest represent the poles on which the Spenserian system turns. A central problem in the *Faerie Queene* (it is also a central problem in Chaucer and Milton) is the reconciliation of fertility and order, love and law. But here we see these powers cooperating harmoniously in a cycle which brings man and natural things to their perfection. This—and much more—is summed up in the figure of Astraea.

Spenser tells us in Book v that Justice ruled man and nature as they were first created:

> Peace vniuersall rayn'd mongst men and beasts,
> And all things freely grew out of the ground:
> Iustice sate high ador'd with solemne feasts,
> And to all people did diude her dred beheasts.
>
> (v.Proem.9.6–9)

But when the world fell from this perfection, Astraea departed. Now she returns, led by August.[24] This second coming of Justice at the harvest season suggests that greater harvest, that final judgment, of which the season is a type. But the golden age which finally begins with that act of judgment has already begun for Christians in the Incarnation, in an act of love. This too Astraea signifies, for in her return, the renaissance believed that Virgil had seen the coming of Messiah: "Iam redit et Virgo; redeunt Saturnia regna." In that event the Christmas psalm proclaims that law and love are reconciled: mercy and truth are met together; justice and peace have kissed each other. The function of Astraea in the cycle of the months is clear. She stands for the advent of the divine Love, the divine Justice into our world of history, the presence of God in the beginning and end and in the midst of times. So August prepares us for December.

For human love and human justice and human labor are not sufficient to their end. The center must intervene in the circle, the timeless come into time. It is the Incarnation which gives meaning to the cycle of time and direction to man's striving. All things would stray to their confusion, as Boethius writes, but that God's purpose draws them back, "by love retorned," to their source and goal. So the circle is made perfect: "Alle thinges seken ayen to hir propre cours, and alle thynges rejoysen hem of hir retornyge ayen to hir nature." [25] Thus Spenser shows us the Incarnation not in itself but in man's joyous response to it: December forgets the year's labors and the cold, "His Sauiors birth his mind so much did glad." Winter wins in the order of time. In January and February we see the triumph of the cold—tribulation and the end of life. But behind the triumph of death, and after the end of time, a greater year begins. There can by definition be no symbol for that final spring in the procession of the months; we glimpse it only in the last stanza of the poem.

Spenser's vision of time embraces its entire course from beginning to end. The six days of creation are repeated in the six ages of history: the sixth age is the period from the Incarnation to the present, and thus the birth of Christ occurs proportionally in history at almost precisely the same point as in Spenser's year.[26] January and February are the age we know, a wintry and declining time of tribulation and death. But we can look forward from the sixth age to the seventh, the great sabbath of God's rest, and looking back we can survey and understand the whole pattern of God's redemptive plan. The circle, like the zodiac, is the emblem of perfection; it is also a symbol of eternity. In the circle of Spenser's calendar, with its counterpoint of labors and virtues, we see the eternal purpose incarnate in time.[27]

But revelation demands response. The plough and hatchet which January and February carry remind us of our obligation to bring the golden age to pass. This ethical lesson is repeated even in the signs of the zodiac. December's shaggy-bearded goat is that with which Amalthea nourished another infant god, and no doubt similar meanings lurk in other zodiacal signs. But more obvious is the fact that several are fertility symbols (fish, flood, bull). Others are dangerous or evil (lion, scorpion, crab). These "eyressh bestes" are ridden or led—and hence controlled— by the human figures of the months like July:

> Vpon a Lyon raging yet with ire
> He boldly rode and made him to obay . . .[28]

This stress on order and control persists in the stanzas on Day and Night, and those on the Hours, who in spite of their loveliness were "Virgins all, and loue eschewed" lest they slight their duties at heaven's gate

> Which they did dayly watch, and nightly wake
> By euen turnes, ne euer did their charge forsake.

Duty and regularity, responsibility and discipline: the recurrent themes are unmistakable. Even Death is insubstantial; the reality is Life, "Full of delightfull health and liuely ioy." But this is not the joy of idleness—his are wings "fit to employ."

At this point Jove, who (unlike many critics) has scrutinized the pageant carefully, asserts that if time changes, it also keeps a course, and demands

> who is it (to me tell)
> That *Time* himselfe doth moue and still compell
> To keepe his course? Is not that namely wee . . . ?

His question is echoed and answered by Hooker: "Who [is] the guide of nature but only the God of nature? *In him wee liue, moue, and are.*"[29] Mutabilitie gives a different reply. It should not be read as a tragic revelation of disorder in the heavens, with the new astronomy calling all in doubt. Spenser does not risk stating the graver implications of his theme so near its resolution: for that we must turn to the Proem of Book v. Mutabilitie's gleeful allusions to Sir Saturn and Dan Jove and Venus, "that goodly Paragone," give her speech a playfullness which prevents our taking the indictment seriously. Spenser's real concern is to disable the astrological notion of the stars as fate: their eccentricities cause star-gazers to "damne their lying bookes." Moreover, Jove is a mortal, born on earth. In other words, the stars are parts of the natural creation; they influence it only as agents of a higher power. And as Mutabilitie turns to that higher power, her tone, with its triumphant hybris, should warn us that her downfall is at hand.

Nature delivers her verdict in a stanza and a half. No more is needed: the evidence which Mutabilitie presents refutes her. All things change, but they change according to a providential law, the law of love which guides them to the perfection of their first estate. Thus they undo the fall, the work of Mutabilitie. The symbolic months represent the values which direct the labors of the rest: Love, Justice, Chastity, and Holiness, the virtues triumphant throughout the *Faerie Queene*.[30] Thus through the labors and disciplines of change, the creation prepares itself for

> that same time when no more *Change* shall be,
> But stedfast rest of all things firmely stayd
> Vpon the pillours of Eternity. . . .

For labor and change are not the ultimate realities, and Spenser's emblem has another meaning. To the Middle Ages and the

Renaissance, the cycle of months suggested the vanity of temporal things no less than their purpose and their order. The power of Spenser's emblem is in part this paradox: it inculcates both commitment and withdrawal. As the figures of the months glide by, we feel their transience as well as their constancy, and we are prepared, half-consciously, for the last stanzas, in which Spenser turns from change and toil to a vision of rest with God. The labor and the rest are not opposed: for the rest is the motive of the toil. "There remaineth . . . a rest to the people of God," writes Paul, "Let us labour, therefore, to entre into the rest. . . ."[31] In the two stanzas of Canto 8, the laborer looks up from his work to its reward, and in the last change in this poem of changes, we move from time to eternity, from action to contemplation.

The developing concepts of Mutabilitie and Nature give to the Cantos their intellectual action: by a kind of ultimate decorum they *enact* the meaning of change and constancy by the steady development and definition of these concepts. Here the very numbering of the Cantos is suggestive.[32] In Canto 6, the sixth age of trial and confusion, Mutabilitie appears to mean flux, disorder, and decay. But in the next canto, the pageant of the months reveals the beauty of constancy within the wheel of change. This is the seventh canto of the seventh book, and the number—itself a symbol of God's immutability and of eternal rest—recalls the stability and repose which completed the labors of creation and pronounced it good. Then, in the eighth canto, we look beyond creation and its weeks to the sabbath which is both the seventh day of rest and the eighth day of resurrection, the glory of which Gloriana's feast is but a type.[33] In the stead-

fast brightness of eternity, the radiance of the months seems
dark indeed. There is a suggestive parallel in the "Hymne of
Heauenly Beautie." There we behold God's image in the mirror
of his work, rising in contemplation from the beauty of earth
and sea up to the heavens and the fixed stars. Finally we behold
the face of Wisdom herself; then—and only then—do we realize
that earthly beauty is meaningless compared to this. It is the
vision of "that soueraine light" which "loathing brings / Of this
vile world, and these gay seeming things." [34] Thus in Canto 8,
Spenser can echo the claim of Mutabilitie herself, declaring that
he loathes this state of life so tickle where "all that moueth, doth
in *Change* delight." These lines have often been read as expres-
sions of personal disillusionment and despair. But it is important
to realize that here, as elsewhere in the opening stanzas of a book
or canto, Spenser speaks in the role of the Poet, the Narrator,
the Presenter, that his sentiments on these occasions are dictated
by decorum and serve to define or emphasize his theme.[35]
Here, extolling the divine changelessness, the poet repudiates all
change. His naïve dismay at the prospect of a world of transience
and toil is not intended to define our response to what has gone
before but to introduce what follows. It directs us towards the
final vision of a transcendant stability and repose, just as the
conventional wording, the lapsing, hesitant rhythms, and feminine
rhymes of the first stanza prepare us for the superb climax of
the final lines. This vision does not cancel the beauty that has
gone before, but offers a final qualifying perspective on it. The
revelation of a transfigured nature is at the center of the Mutabilitie Cantos, and its meaning is declared by a higher authority
than the poet. At the end of the seventh canto, Nature has put

aside her veil, for the creatures are described as "looking in her face." As she pronounces sentence, we see the purpose and meaning of Nature, no longer in the dark glass of her created works or in the veiled allegory of the months, but explicitly and simply, face to face. The reader, like Solomon, has been instructed by Wisdom herself in "the true knowledge of the things that are . . . The beginning and the end, & the middes of the times: how the times alter, and the changes of the seasons, The course of the yere, the situacion of the starres." [36]

Read in this way, the Mutabilitie Cantos take their due place as Spenser's "Legend of Constancy." As decorum requires, we find the virtue of the book exemplified in many aspects of the poem. We find it symbolized in the circular garlands which deck Molanna and her father Mole, in the star Vesper which guides the mutable moon in its course, "And ioy to weary wandring trauailers did lend"—note the pun on "trauailers." We find it in allusions like the marriage of Peleus and Thetis, for Peleus won his divine bride by clinging to her through all her changing shapes. We see it in Jove settling himself to meet his foe (his sitting posture, writes Abraham Fraunce, betokens his immutability),[37] and in the aspect of Nature herself, "Still moouing, yet vnmoued from her sted." We watch it prevailing in the action, in the cycles which restore Molanna to Fanchin and bring a goddess once again to Arlo Hill. Thus the Cantos exemplify and define constancy, and it is not what we supposed, for Spenser has the power of genius to surprise. It is not, in this world at least, a power "contrayr" to Mutabilitie. It is a purpose persisting through mutability, redeeming it. It combines the energy of love with the stability of law; it is not a denial of change but a direction for work. We hardly need the rest of the seventh book to exemplify its virtue. For the central emblem of the Cantos is the cycle of twelve months, which for Bersuire symbolize the twelve virtues or works of the just man. And the *Faerie Queene* itself, aiming to "fashion a gentleman or noble person in vertuous and gentle discipline," is also planned as a cycle of the twelve private moral virtues. Each knight repeats this cycle in twelve cantos, beginning as the bare title of a virtue, but laboring till it becomes his very nature. The virtue of the seventh book is not without a champion, for each of Spenser's knights in turn becomes the type of constancy, quitting the Eden of the Faerie Queene to work his own perfection in the realms of Mutabilitie.

A . K E N T H I E A T T

The Daughters of Horus: Order
in the Stanzas of *Epithalamion*

IN A RECENT BOOK [1] I have attempted to show that Spenser's
Epithalamion, in addition to what it has always been for its readers, is a tissue of time-symbolism in which the movements of the
sun through the day and the year are indicated. The claims of
this book, insofar as they relate to the present essay, may be thus
summarized:

The ultimate reference of this symbolism is to that order in
mutability which is the fit mirror in time of the changeless order
of eternity; that is to say, the order symbolically represented in
Epithalamion is the same one which Spenser celebrates in a
different way in the Mutability Cantos. The appropriateness of
this symbolism to a marriage-ode depends on the well-known
estimate of the human race in the realm of time as an ordered
succession of forms (as in *FQ* III.6)—a kind of dance—in which
the regenerative aspect is institutionalized in marriage. Although
it has long been recognized that all aspects of these ideas, taken
singly, are parts of the Spenserian *Denkwelt,* it is only in *Epithalamion* that Spenser has given so striking a poetic formula-
tion to them in combination, in terms of the parallel between

the cyclical character of time as measured by the heavens and the cyclical existence of humanity.

This, so far, is the general case. Some of the devices by which I claim this symbolism is carried through in *Epithalamion* are numerical; for most of these the evidence is so nearly complete that their existence in the poem will not, perhaps, be seriously questioned. One other device, however, is not primarily numerical and will be, or ought to be, independently investigated. This device is less novel, poetically more interesting for its own sake, and probably more susceptible to interpretive error and exaggeration than any of the others. What this device amounts to, as I describe it,[2] is that, of *Epithalamion*'s twenty-four stanzas (each representing an hour) the first twelve are made to match the following twelve, one for one, by the use of metaphorical parallels and covert conceits in a way well-known in Spenserian allegory and in Elizabethan poetry in general. The rationale which I ascribe to this division is that by it Spenser indicates the four seasonal divisions of the year. Of the twenty-four sidereal hours, twelve are above and twelve below the horizon at the spring equinox; at the equinox of autumn their positions are reversed. At the summer solstice in Ireland (the day and place of the marriage) sixteen and a fraction sidereal hours are above the horizon, and seven and a fraction below, as is symbolized by the change of refrain from positive to negative in the seventeenth stanza of the poem (where night arrives); but by the device of the matching stanzas this division serves for the winter solstice as well, when the positions of the sidereal hours are again reversed.

Evidence for this matching of the stanzas, twelve and twelve,

undoubtedly exists. I have reproduced it in my book. I believe
that the parallels cited there generally invite conviction. But our
ignorance of the statistical probabilities upon which the degree
of likelihood of this part of my theory ultimately depends makes
it most desirable that an independent investigator should test
my contention by attempting an alternative matching of these
stanzas. If it succeeds as well as mine, something is wrong with
the theory: either my contention about matching is entirely
fanciful, or Spenser's intention extends only to an occasional
metaphorical echoing of earlier matter (in a way not unknown
in others of his works), not to a completely symmetrical scheme.[8]

Meanwhile, however, I continue to regard this particular feature
of the poem as what I have already described: a matching of
stanza-hours, one by one, as between the first and second halves
of the poem. What I propose to do now is to investigate, more
fully than I have done in my book, the quality of this matching
in two pairs of stanzas in which the essential correspondences
are more occult than they are in most of the other stanza-pairs
(in these latter Spenser is enabled by his scheme to play on the
contrasts between day and night on the day of the marriage).
The gain which I anticipate from this exercise, apart from a just
estimate of one kind of poetic achievement in *Epithalamion,* is
that for once we may measure accurately how far Spenser's
allusiveness extends, and in what sense it is multiple and polyse-
mous. For once (I claim) we have Spenser imprisoned in his
own covert structural intentions and working to very close toler-
ances—in each case two stanzas or less than forty lines. Allowing
for the difference in genre between this poem and most of his
other work, we may still claim that demonstrated multiplicity

and elegance of figurative correspondence here would allow us
to affirm more confidently the presence of such qualities in his
other works, in the face of the usual lay claim that his allegory
is a simple logical structure with arbitrary and unmeaning "poetic" decorations.

It is only fair to admit, however, that I may be wrong, and
that the validity of my case rests on the assumption that Spenser
intended to match his stanzas in the way I have described. If
this assumption were to prove generally unacceptable in terms of
the demonstration which I have attempted in my book, it is
difficult to see how the neat poetic equivalences which I suggest
below could be supposed to provide additional proof for my
theory, for it is a fact of research that for almost any preliminary
assumption corroborative details can be found; the chief task is
to show initially that the assumption is necessary.

II

Stanzas 1 and 13, which follow, are the first of the two stanza-
pairs to be investigated here.[4]

> Ye learned sisters which have oftentimes
> Beene to me ayding, others to adorne:
> Whom ye thought worthy of your gracefull rymes,
> That even the greatest did not greatly scorne
> To heare theyr names sung in your simple layes,
> But joyed in theyr prayse
> And when ye list your owne mishaps to mourne
> Which death, or love, or fortunes wreck did rayse,

Your string could soone to sadder tenor turne,
And teach the woods and waters to lament
Your doleful dreriment.
Now lay those sorrowful complaints aside,
And having all your heads with girland crownd,
Helpe me mine owne loves prayses to resound,
Ne let the same of any be envide:
So Orpheus did for his own bride,
So I unto my selfe alone will sing,
The woods shall to me answer and my Eccho ring.

(ll. 1–18)

Behold whiles she before the altar stands
Hearing the holy priest that to her speakes
And blesseth her with his two happy hands
How the red roses flush up in her cheekes,
And the pure snow with goodly vermill stayne,
Like crimsin dyde in grayne,
That even th' angels which continually,
About the sacred Altare doe remaine,
Forget their service and about her fly,
Ofte peeping in her face that seems more fayre,
The more they on it stare.
But her sad eyes still fastened on the ground,
Are governed with goodly modesty,
That suffers not one looke to glaunce awry,
Which may let in a little thought unsownd.
Why blush ye love to give to me your hand,

> The pledge of all our band?
> Sing ye sweet Angels, Alleluya sing,
> That all the woods may answere and your eccho ring.
>
> (ll. 223–41)

I have already described [5] the main feature of parallelism here: as Spenser does at least twice elsewhere, he creates in these two stanzas a parallel by contrast between the activities of muses and angels as singers of the praises of a favored female. The muses are to turn from their other activities to help Spenser sing the praises of his beloved: the angels undergo a similar shift of their attention (ll. 229–33) and receive from him a similar injunction to sing the praises of his beloved (ll. 240–41). Generally speaking, the parallel here involves a commonplace of Elizabethan poetry: that there is an association between poetic or vatic inspiration and divine inspiration.

There is, however, another kind of parallelism in this pair of stanzas. To begin with, we know that another commonplace of Elizabethan poetry is its power to immortalize mortal men. For Spenser the muses naturally enter in here as well: for example, he says of them, in *The Ruines of Time,* in a development of the myth of Orpheus:

> And they, for pittie of the sad Wayment,
> Which *Orpheus* for *Eurydice* did make,
> Her back againe to life sent for his sake.
>
> (ll. 390–92)

Orpheus is mentioned, as we know, in stanza 1 of *Epithalamion.* His role there seems to be a more extensive one than is suggested by the two lines,

> So Orpheus did for his own bride,
> So I unto my selfe alone will sing. . . .   (ll. 16–17)

For one thing, we are told earlier in the stanza that Spenser had
employed his muse on sadder subjects, as of course Orpheus had
done. The lines go:

> Your string could soone to sadder tenor turne
> And teach the woods and waters to lament . . .
>
> (ll. 9–10)

Orpheus, too, had controlled the woods and waters by his lamen-
tations for Eurydice; in fact Spenser says as much in *Virgils
Gnat*:

> For the swift running rivers still did stand,
> And the wilde beasts their furie did withhold,
> To follow *Orpheus* musicke through the land:
> And th'Okes deep grounded in the earthly molde
> Did move, as if they could him understand;
> And the shrill woods, which were of sense bereav'd,
> Through their hard barke his silver sound receav'd.
>
> (ll. 450–56)

But after that, *Virgils Gnat* goes on to tell us, Orpheus had sung
to the infernal powers for his love, as Spenser sang to himself
alone (at l. 17 in *Epithalamion*) in praise of his love. Of Orpheus this section of *Virgils Gnat* tells us first that by the power
of his song he delayed Cynthia in her nightly journey and then,
of him:

> The same was able with like lovely lay
> The Queene of hell to move as easily,

> To yeeld *Eurydice* unto here fere,
> Backe to be borne, though it unlawfull were.
>
> (ll. 461-64)

And in the process of extracting Eurydice from hell Orpheus was, of course, subject to enmity: in *An Hymne of Love* we have:

> . . . *Orpheus* daring to provoke the yre
> Of damned fiends, to get his love retyre. . . .
>
> (ll. 234-35)

Eurydice well knew this quality in these fiends; according to *Virgils Gnat,*

> She (Ladie) having well before aprooved
> The feendes to be too cruell and severe.
>
> (ll. 465-66)

Now, the effect of all these things—the lamentation affecting woods and water; the subsequent turn to the celebration of the beloved, with which the muses are associated; and the subjection to enmity—is that there is a parallel between Orpheus and Spenser which seems to enter into the meaning of stanza 1 of *Epithalamion,* lines 9-18, even affecting the content of the memorable refrain. We need to reread these lines with these points in mind:

> Your string could soone to sadder tenor turne,
> And teach the woods and waters to lament
> Your doleful dreriment.
> Now lay those sorrowful complaints aside,

> And having all your heads with girland crownd,
> Helpe me mine owne loves prayses to resound,
> Ne let the same of any be envide:
> So Orpheus did for his own bride,
> So I unto my selfe alone will sing,
> The woods shall to me answer and my Eccho ring.

As Orpheus and Spenser, associated with the muses, had influenced nature to lament, so now Spenser, singing to himself, will also make the woods resound with joy, as Orpheus, singing to the powers of hell, had influenced them. In both cases fear of inimical powers is expressed. The "woods and waters" perhaps look forward to the influence which Spenser tells the muses to exert over river- and forest-nymphs in stanza 3:

> Bring with you all the Nymphes that you can heare
>   [that is, "that can hear you"]
> Both of the rivers and the forrests greene: . . .
>
> (ll. 37–38)

But we have not yet touched on what we started with: the connection here between this material in stanza 1, related in one way to Orpheus, and other material in the matching stanza 13. In *Virgils Gnat* Spenser summarizes the crucial point in the story of Orpheus and Eurydice in this way:

> And sad *Eurydice* thence now no more
> Must turne to life, but there detained bee,
> For looking back, being forbid before:
> Yet was the guilt thereof, *Orpheus,* in thee . . .
>
> (ll. 433–36)

For Spenser knows, of course, that it was not Eurydice who
looked back. He says a little later in *Virgils Gnat* that she

> Observ'd th' appointed way, as her behooved,
> Ne ever did her ey-sight turne arere,
> Ne ever spake, ne cause of speaking mooved. . . .
>
> (ll. 467–69)

The important point, however, is that in stanza 13 of *Epithalamion* Spenser's bride behaves in much the same way:

> But her sad eyes still fastened on the ground,
> Are governed with goodly modesty,
> That suffers not one looke to glaunce awry,
> Which may let in a little thought unsownd.
>
> (ll. 234–37)

The parallel, then, between the two poets is (as I claim) ex-
tended to the two brides, but again with a difference, as between old and new dispensations. It is on this parallel by contrast that the matching of the two stanzas in part depends. Eurydice, environed by cruel, severe, damned fiends, somewhat like
Guyon in the Cave of Mammon, is doomed, because

> . . . cruell *Orpheus,* thou much crueller,
> Seeking to kisse her, brok'st the Gods decree,
> And thereby mad'st her ever damn'd to be.
>
> (*Virgils Gnat,* ll. 470–72)

Spenser's bride, however, is in a different position. It is angels,
not fiends, that fly about her and peep in her face; and the holy
priest blesses her with his two happy (*i.e.,* "felicitous," "for-

tunate") hands. It is no wonder, then, that Spenser need not accuse himself of cruelty in love or of impiety when he asks her, "Why blush ye love to give to me your hand, / The pledge of all our band?" Circumstances alter cases.

Actually, it may be that Spenser by his request for the bride's hand, and by her reaction, is recalling a passage from Eurydice's farewell to Orpheus at the end of Virgil's *Georgics:*

> . . . En iterum crudelia retro
> Fata vocant, conditque natantia lumina somnus.
> Iamque vale: feror ingenti, circumdata nocte,
> Invalidasque tibi tendens, heu non tua, palmas.
>
> (iv.495–98)

> Once more the cruel fates call me back, and sleep veils my swimming eyes. And now farewell! I am borne away swathed in night's vast pall, stretching towards thee powerless hands —thine, alas, no more.

"Invalidas . . . palmas," "heu non tua"; "Why blush ye love to give to me your hand, / The pledge of all our band?" The contrast is a moving one.

To sum up: we cannot claim to have expressed here the total meaning of these two stanzas; for one thing we have not touched upon their very important surface meanings, which concern simply the praise of Spenser's beloved on their marriage day. But associated with these surface matters is another meaning, revolving about the conception of creativity in which the poetic is set beside the divine. The classical myth chiefly suited to express the poet's command over an outward nature—the myth of Orpheus—is evoked to communicate, incidentally, Spenser's conception of himself as belonging to the vatic line, but mainly to express the quality of the blessed love here being celebrated over against the doomed and distraught love of the less fortunate poet.

The suitability of these juxtapositions to the rest of the poem is worthy of note: *Epithalamion* is, *par excellence,* the work of Spenser's in which his favorite antithesis about love—its gentleness and its cruelty—runs its course completely on the side of the first of these members: it is a poem from which misfortune, often taken into account, is yet always banished. Furthermore, the comparison between the poetic and divine powers of creativity is very much to the point: *Epithalamion,* as I believe I have shown in my book, creates a day and a year by the same artifices of mutability in sameness—the daily and annual apparent motions of the sun—as the divine will makes use of, so that the poem may, more literally than any other work, assert the claim made in its last line: ". . . for short time an endlesse moniment," meaning, in one sense, a monument to time because the poem re-creates the substance of time itself. One must note as well, however, the humility before the divine which is one of the many other meanings this line conveys: ". . . for short time an endlesse moniment" may also mean that *Epithalamion* is endless only for the period of short time; it is not, like God's work at the conclusion of the Mutability Cantos, ". . . stayd / Upon the pillours of eternity."

III

The second pair of matching stanzas to be reviewed here are stanzas 3 and 15:

Bring with you all the Nymphes that you can heare
Both of the rivers and the forrests greene:
And of the sea that neighbours to her neare,
Al with gay girlands goodly wel beseene.
And let them also with them bring in hand
Another gay girland
For my fayre love of lillyes and of roses,
Bound truelove wize with a blew silke riband.
And let them make great store of bridale poses,
And let them eeke bring store of other flowers
To deck the bridale bowers.
And let the ground whereas her foot shall tread,
For feare the stones her tender foot should wrong
Be strewed with fragrant flowers all along,
And diapred lyke the discolored mead.
Which done, doe at her chamber dore awayt,
For she will waken strayt,
The whiles doe ye this song unto her sing,
The woods shall to you answer and your Eccho ring.

(ll. 37–55)

Ring ye the bels, ye yong men of the towne,
And leave your wonted labors for this day:
This day is holy; doe ye write it downe,
That ye for ever it remember may.
This day the sunne is in his chiefest hight,
With Barnaby the bright,
From whence declining daily by degrees,
He somewhat loseth of his heat and light,

When once the Crab behind his back he sees.
But for this time it ill ordained was,
To chose the longest day in all the yeare,
And shortest night, when longest fitter weare:
Yet never day so long, but late would passe.
Ring ye the bels, to make it weare away,
And bonefiers make all day,
And daunce about them, and about them sing:
That all the woods may answer, and your eccho ring.

Again, the correspondences are among the more occult in the
system of stanza-matching which I have posited. The correspondences which I have already claimed [6] in these two stanzas
are the following:

1. In stanza 3 the muses are told to gather nymphs and to confer special duties upon them for the day; in stanza 15, the poet
imposes other special duties for the day on the young men of the
town.

2. In stanza 15 (and only there) we learn that this day is
Saint Barnabas' Day, for which, on unimpeachable and unani-
mous independent evidence, the sole folk-activity in sixteenth-
century and later England was flower-gathering by women for
the decoration of churches; in stanza 3, the chief activity of the
nymphs is flower-gathering and flower-arrangement for the wedding (ll. 41–51). (It will be useful to remember in a later connection that the nymphs are all to wear garlands and that they
are to bring with them another garland for the bride.)

3. The repeated injunction to the young men in stanza 15 to
ring the bells, and specifically line 274, "Ring ye the bels, to make

it [*i.e.,* the day] weare away," relates to the injunction to the
muses in stanza 3, "doe ye this song unto her sing" (l. 54), for all
save the last of the stanzas, or stanza-hours, of *Epithalamion*
end with the word "ring"; the singing of the song may thus be
thought of as wearing away the day, as does bell-ringing.

Another meaning of the word "ring," however, leads to certain further reflections. No other two stanzas in the poem contain so many references to circular enclosures. A garland, for instance, was, for Spenser as for us, a ring of flowers. He says of
Belphoebe, for example, "All her Nymphes did like a girlond
her enclose" (*FQ* iii.6.19.9), and he compares a round dance to a
garland, and calls it a ring, in a passage apparently celebrating
the same lady as does *Epithalamion*:

> All they without were raunged in a ring,
> And daunced round; but in the midst of them
> Three other ladies did both daunce and sing,
> The whilest the rest them round about did hemme,
> And like a girlond did in compasse stemme:
> And in the middest of those same three, was placed
> Another Damzell, as a precious gemme
> Amidst a ring most richly well enchaced,
> That with her goodly presence all the rest much graced.
>   (*FQ* vi.10.12)

We are told not only that the dance around this lady was like
a garland, but also (a little later) that she in fact wore a rosy
garland on her head (vi.10.14.5) as the dancers pelted her with
flowers.

Thus, for Spenser, all the garlands of the passage in stanza 3

of *Epithalamion* would be circular, ring-like objects. The nymphs
are to be

> Al with gay girlands goodly wel beseene.
> And let them also with them bring in hand
> Another gay girland
> For my fayre love of lillyes and of roses . . .

(ll. 40–43)

Furthermore, the young men of the town in the matching stanza
are to build bonfires all day, "And daunce about them, and about
them sing" (l. 276), somewhat like the ladies dancing and singing about Colin Clout's beloved on Mount Acidale, in the passage
quoted above from *The Faerie Queene*. There is only one way
to dance around a bonfire, and that is in a ring, usually with
hands joined. Furthermore, there are the three instances of the
word "ring" in this stanza and the repeated "rings" suggested
by the muses' singing of *Epithalamion* in stanza 3. Why all this
circularity?

References to two circles of another kind in stanza 15 may be
the key. This stanza is, in fact, in many ways a key stanza to the
puzzle of the whole poem. It is the only one that mentions the
two movements of the sun which the total poem at one level
symbolizes: the daily apparent westward motion with the fixed
stars, the yearly apparent eastward motion along the Zodiac. It
is the only stanza, as well, which refers to the shortest and longest days in the year, which, in turn, are symbolized by one of the
ways in which the poem is divided. The stanza also plays on the
contrast "shortest-longest." In addition, the stanza itself is the
shortest of the long stanzas (*i.e.,* of the regular stanzas, exclusive

of the short envoy), but it includes a long line where, according to the scheme of almost all the other stanzas, a short line is expected. This line (271) includes a punning reference to its own length: "To chose the longest day in all the yeare." What is chiefly relevant here, however, are simply the references to the simultaneous motions of the sun—forward, through the day, and backward, like a crab, about one degree a day to complete the circle of the year in 365 days. It is by this latter motion, of course, that we also have shorter and longer days. The whole passage goes as follows:

> This day the sunne is in his chiefest hight,
> With Barnaby the bright,
> From whence declining daily by degrees,
> He somewhat loseth of his heat and light,
> When once the Crab behind his back he sees.
> But for this time it ill ordained was,
> To chose the longest day in all the yeare,
> And shortest night, when longest fitter weare:
> Yet never day so long, but late would passe.
> Ring ye the bels, to make it weare away . . .
>
> (ll. 265–74)

The two apparent motions of the sun are, of course, circular, ring-like.

In the midst of the passages in *FQ* vi which we have quoted —the ones connecting circular dances, garlands, rings, and apparently the same lady as the bride in *Epithalamion* (this lady having her head engarlanded and being pelted with flowers)— we have in addition an astronomical image as lovely as its mythology and star-lore are inaccurate. After the dancers have been compared to a garland around her, and after she herself has been compared to a precious jewel in a ring, but before we are told that she wears a garland, she and those about her are compared to the constellation of Ariadne's Crown and to the stars which Spenser loosely and ambiguously imagines as circling about it, as though it were the North Star:

> Looke how the Crowne, which *Ariadne* wore
> Upon her yvory forehead that same day,
> That *Theseus* her unto his bridale bore,
> When the bold *Centaures* made that bloudy fray
> With the fierce *Lapithes,* which did them dismay,
> Being now placed in the firmament,
> Through the bright heaven doth her beames display,
> And is unto the starres an ornament,
> Which round about her move in order excellent.
>
> Such was the beauty of this goodly band . . .
>
> (VI.10.13, 14.1)

Now, this is about a marriage. The lady to whom the comparison applies is almost surely the one who is celebrated in *Epithalamion*. I suggest, on the basis of this and what has gone before, that Spenser was operating, in the matching stanzas 3 and 15 of *Epithalamion,* with the same images and the same imaginative ordering as he did in the passages from *FQ* VI which I have quoted: in *Epithalamion,* garlands, rings, ring-dances, and the revolution of heavenly bodies about a common center become for him the image of his great creative gesture—the image of the sun tracing his circles around the earth and imposing in the day, the seasons, and the year that eternity in mutability upon which all created life depends, and which is, as well, an abstract of human life, particularly at the high point of marriage.

This, then, concludes our examination. What I claim that we should see in the two pairs of stanzas here dealt with is not only the delightful, easy, freshly flowing *facundia* which has been so long admired in this poem, but also a densely and deftly woven, flexible, economical web of associations and allusions, ample enough to contain within the bounds of the marriage day the resources of a profound reflection. The parallelism here described is a feat of the syncretic imagination—not mine, as I believe, but Spenser's. If the claims made here are just, we may trust more fully the view that the Spenser of *The Faerie Queene* and of the *Hymnes* is not, in the main, the facile decorator of a given framework of concepts, but a poet whose every image is considered with an eye to something beyond sensuous impact—to an evolving, felt pattern of meaning, multifariously interconnected. This deserves emphasis, although *Epithalamion* by itself is object enough for our reflections, being, as it is, one of the greatest and most beautiful artifacts of our language.

The Use of Conventions in Spenser's Minor Poems

WHEN I HAPPENED to mention, at a lunch table at the Huntington Library, that I was working on Spenser's minor poems, a young scholar across from me, who is interested in Elizabethan poetry and who has published articles on Spenser, made the remark that the trouble with Spenser's minor poems is that they are so *dull*. Up to that point it hadn't occurred to me to consider whether they were dull or not—as poems; I was studying them to see what material they offered for an investigation that interests me very much—the investigation of what major poetic conventions the Elizabethans used, what meaning these conventions had for the poets and their readers, and what modes of expression arose from the shared understanding of these conventions and meanings. Such study I had found rewarding in a book published eight years ago,[1] and I wished to extend it.

Now a poem may be dull for any one of a number of reasons; if it is dull because of a lack of talent in the poet, certainly nothing can be done about it. A minor poet once complained to Oscar Wilde about the failure of his poems to attract any attention. "It's a conspiracy of silence, Oscar," he said, "what shall I do?" "Join it," said Wilde, "join it." If, however, a poem seems dull to us because the conventions upon which it is based have lost meaning for us, or acquired other meanings, then the kind of investigation I propose may have some value in restoring these old works, removing some of the dark varnish that has obscured their colors and allowing us to see them afresh.

The most familiar example will illustrate what I mean. Dr. Johnson's notorious critique of *Lycidas* may, as a whole, be inexplicable. How are we to account for a taste which finds in *Lycidas* "the diction . . . harsh, the rhymes uncertain, and the numbers unpleasing"? [2] But we can, I think account for the later part of Johnson's criticism as a failure to see the relevant meaning in a convention. "In this poem there is no nature, for there is no truth; there is no art, for there is nothing new. Its form is that of a pastoral: easy, vulgar, and therefore disgusting; whatever images it can supply are long ago exhausted; and its inherent improbability always forces dissatisfaction on the mind." This view is of course a famous oddity, a warning to critics of their fallibility. Johnson actually thought that no man could have fancied that he read *Lycidas* with pleasure, had he not known the author. Yet John Crowe Ransom in our own time has called it "A Poem Nearly Anonymous." [3] The convention of the pastoral elegy has been understood and validated, most significantly in an essay by George Norlin first published in 1911.[4] No one need have now the difficulty with *Lycidas* which Dr. Johnson had.

I should also perhaps remark that the kind of study I have in mind is to be sharply distinguished from source study. Much laborious work has been done on Spenser's sources; the notes to the Variorum edition attest to this. But the study of a poet's use of conventions is in a way almost opposite to source study, since when a poet is writing in a convention he is aware of more than one example of the convention he is using. He feels the meaning of that convention and is therefore more significantly guided by it than he is by the wording of any particular example of it. Again, *Lycidas* is a rather obvious instance.

In my book on Elizabethan poetry I discussed *The Shepheardes Calender* and *Colin Clouts Come Home Againe* as part of my treatment of the pastoral eclogue. I tried to establish the thesis that for the Elizabethans pastoral was not, as most modern critics had assumed, an escape from life but a criticism of life and an assertion of the values of *otium* against the values associated with the aspiring mind. In the pastoral eclogue Spenser had a highly conventional form appropriate for his first ambitious attempt to create a new English poetry and equally appropriate for the critical survey of the court and his culture in the time of the poet's maturity. I reached the conclusion that *The Shepheardes Calender* is a very considerable work of art, demonstrating brilliantly that English verse is capable of the most varied and complex effects, all within a traditional mode which had a general European acceptance. I do not know how many readers followed me and agree with that conclusion, but I shall not attempt to defend it further, and I shall leave *The Shepheardes Calender* out of consideration here. I also treated the *Amoretti* and made an attempt to characterize Spenser's sonnets more precisely by showing how they differ in intention, technique, and effect from other sonnet cycles within the convention, such as those of Sidney, Shakespeare, Daniel, and Drayton. I am happy not to have to deal further with the *Amoretti* here, but to leave that subject in the capable hands of Professor Martz.

I propose to focus my attention on four poems: *Muiopotmos, Daphnaida, Epithalamion,* and *Prothalamion.* In approaching these poems I will assume my conclusions based upon *The Shepheardes Calender* and the *Amoretti*—that Spenser was a conscious artist, well aware of the conventions and interested in using them in English to demonstrate the marvelous possibilities of that language, but fundamentally independent and experimental. Whether he succeeds or fails artistically, Spenser seems always insistent upon handling a convention in such a way as to leave upon it the unmistakable stamp of his own mind and style.

I do not take the old-fashioned view that conventions are forced upon the poet and hamper him, so that the critic must be constantly apologetic about the conventions and urge the reader to put up with them for the sake of an occasional break-through into originality. Instead I suppose that the conventions are the primary materials with which the poet works as an artist; this material is neither attractive nor unattractive in itself—everything depends upon what is done with it. I do feel rather old-fashioned, however, when I read Derek Traversi's discussion of Spenser in the Penguin *Guide to English Literature.* He maintains that Spenser exhibits a certain amount of virtuosity, finish, and style, but that on the whole he is a failure because he uses decayed conventions and does not use them very well. Spenser's adaption of the pastoral convention in *The Shepheardes Calender,* for instance, "implies an effort, more or less imposed by circumstances, to evade a direct approach to delicate realities." [5] Mr. Traversi suggests that "already there is a perilous lack of root in this convention (the pastoral). Those whose way of life

has become remote from the real soil cannot be expected to pre-
serve for long the veneer of the soil; and that, translated into
social terms, is the meaning of *The Shepheardes Calender*." The
allegorical convention, he goes on to say, was rotten by the time
Spenser chose it for *The Faerie Queene*. "To compare Spenser's
poem, strictly as an allegorical construction, with *Piers Plowman*,
is to be aware of the decay of a convention that had once been
valid and had corresponded to a coherent organization of experience."

I am not going to impose my judgment on conventions, as Dr.
Johnson imposed his on the pastoral elegy. Nor am I going to
plot the life-cycle of a convention and refer to its infancy, adoles-
cence, maturity, senility, and demise. I am merely going to en-
quire into Spenser's handling of conventions in four poems
and see what help this gives me in evaluating him as an
artist.

Muiopotmos, or The Fate of the Butterflie was published in
the volume called *Complaints* (1591), but it has its own title
page dated 1590. It was presumably written not long before. It is
dedicated to Lady Carey, in an epistle signed by Spenser, full of
the usual Elizabethan flattery and self-deprecation but interesting
because the poet beseeches her to take his gift in worth, and in all
things therein *to make a mild construction,* according to her
wonted graciousness. I suppose this means that she is to read no
more into the poem than is there, and perhaps more specifically,
not to suppose it to be a satire or topical poem, like *Mother
Hubberds Tale* and *Virgil's Gnat,* which preceded *Muiopotmos*
in the *Complaints* volume.

Muiopotmos contains many puzzles, and the scholarly com-

mentary on the poem has largely concerned itself with suggesting
answers to these puzzles, the authors often forgetting Spenser's
admonition to make a mild construction. The poem begins as if
it were to be a mock epic:

> I sing of deadly dolorous debate,
> Stir'd vp through wrathfull Nemesis despight,
> Betwixt two mightie ones of great estate,
> Drawne into armes, and proofe of mortall fight,
> Through prowd ambition, and hartswelling hate,
> Whilest neither could the others greater might
> And sdeignfull scorne endure; that from small iarre
> Their wraths at length broke into open warre.

One expects something like the battle of the frogs and the mice,
and the second stanza continues with an invocation to the muse
Melpomene, "the mournfulst Muse of nine." But then the poem
proceeds to tell of Clarion, the butterfly, how he, a fresh and lusty
youth, put on his armor and sallied forth, surveying delectable
gardens, only to be caught in the web of the sinister spider,
Aragnoll, and killed. There is no "deadly dolorous debate," no
"open warre," unless a single stroke by the spider be so considered, no epic battle. However, Spenser does revive the appropriate rhetoric in a stanza just preceding the catastrophe,
and Melpomene is again invoked; the final line in its abruptness
suggests the ending of the Aeneid.

Most of the 440 lines of the poem, however, are devoted to
description of the garden and to the elaboration of two Ovidian
myths which are standard and conventional digressions in an
epyllion. One is the metamorphosis of Astery, to explain the

flowerlike designs in the wings of butterflies; the other is the metamorphosis of Arachne, to explain the notorious malice of spiders: Arachne was the mother of Aragnoll.

The poem has obvious relationships with Chaucer—the mock heroics of *Sir Thopas* and *The Nun's Priest's Tale* hover vaguely in the background, and there is a Chaucerian catalogue of flowers. In style and tone *Muiopotmos* somewhat resembles *Virgil's Gnat,* that translation of the *Culex* which Spenser had done ten years before, in the "raw conceipt" of his youth, to use the terms Spenser applied to the time when he was twenty-seven or twenty-eight years of age. But the most clearly conventional parts of the poem are the two Ovidian digressions.

In the first one Spenser accounts for the beautiful markings in a butterfly's wing by inventing a small and charming metamorphosis. His pretense is that it is legendary, but actually he invents it on the pattern of the story of Cupid and Psyche. One of Venus's nymphs, named Astery, is the most successful of all in gathering flowers; she arouses the envy of the other nymphs, who report falsely that Cupid has been helping her. Venus, afraid of having her son involved in another love affair like that with Psyche which caused so much trouble, changes the nymph Astery into a butterfly, and places on her wings those flowers which had caused her downfall, since when all butterflies carry these designs on their wings.

The legend provides a pleasant prologue to Spenser's elaborate description of the garden; it associates the action with an Ovidian mythological world, and it supplies a kind of mirror-image of the main plot of the poem. It is Astery's fate, through no fault of her own, to be transformed into a butterfly; it is Clarion the butterfly's fate, through no fault of his own, to get caught in the spider's web and be slain.

The second metamorphosis tells the story of Minerva and Arachne from Book Six of Ovid's Metamorphoses. It is introduced to explain the malice of Aragnoll the spider, since he is Arachne's son. Spenser greatly abbreviates Ovid's narrative. In the weaving contest he has Arachne portray only the rape of Europa instead of the twenty-one amours of the gods in Ovid's account. But he adds to the story of Minerva's weaving a detail which is invented to make the mythological digression more relevant. Minerva weaves a butterfly into her picture, and it is the butterfly which is the final triumph of her art. Spenser also changes the ending of the legend; in his version Arachne turns into a spider from envy and grief, whereas Ovid had made the metamorphosis a gift of the goddess to prevent the mortal woman from committing suicide. Spenser by his change relates the legend more closely to his main plot as he uses it to account for Aragnoll's hatred of butterflies.

To Spenser the convention he was using was not a fully fixed and rigid one. It was generally defined by the example of *Virgil's Gnat,* influenced by Chaucer and Ovid, traditional enough to be recognized, but not so fixed in form as the pastoral eclogue. Its trivial subject and light tone gave freedom for pictorial and descriptive effects. The serious episodes are seen in miniature, and the effect is more playful and less satirical than the mock heroic. The poem is a delicate artifact, suitable for presentation to a lady. Its theme is the romantic one so dear to Spenser's heart—the theme of joy and delight which fades and dies as an exemplification of mutability.

What more felicitie can fall to creature
Than to enjoy delight with libertie,
And to be Lord of all the works of Nature,
To raine in th'aire from earth to highest skie,
To feed on flowres, and weeds of glorious feature,
To take what euer thing doth please the eie?
Who rests not pleased with such happines,
Well worthie he to taste of wretchednes.

But what on earth can long abide in state?
Or who can him assure of happie day;
Sith morning faire may bring fowle euening late,
And most mishap the most blisse alter may?
For thousand perills lie in close awaite
About vs daylie, to worke our decay;
That none, except a God, or God him guide,
May them auoyde, or remedie prouide.   (ll. 209–224)

The first two lines were chosen by John Keats to stand on the title page of his first book of poems in 1817, together with a portrait of Spenser.

Because of some puzzles in the poem and because *Virgil's Gnat* is a topical poem, many modern commentators have been tempted to read *Muiopotmos* as an allegory. The interpretations vary. We have been told that the poem is about Spenser and Lady Carey, Ralegh and Essex, Spenser and Burghley, Sidney and Oxford, Burghley and Essex, the defeat of the Armada,[6] and, most recently, The Soul Caught in the Eternal War between Reason and Sensuality.[7] If I were to add to this formidable list, I would be tempted to suggest that *Muiopotmos* is a *prophetic* allegory: that the butterfly represents the scholarly critic who gets caught in the spider-web of extraneous antiquarian, historical, and philosophical learning. But I shall refrain. The tone of the poem, which most of the learned allegorical interpreters ignore, is the first and most important clue to the interpretation, and that tone would almost certainly rule out any heavy philosophical, military, or political allegory. The second clue, I think, comes from Sonnet 71 of *Amoretti,* in which the poet describes his lady's embroidery or "drawn work" as portraying a spider and a bee. It may be that Lady Carey also was interested in sewing; she is the patroness of the poem and Professor Strathmann noticed that there is a record of presenting Queen Elizabeth with a highly embroidered satin garment.[8] I think it is clear that the poem is a light, delicate, *jeu d'esprit* in which Spenser combines elements from Ovid, from a Chaucerian tradition, and from *Virgil's Gnat.* Renwick considered *Muiopotmos* to be "Spenser's most original poem, and that because the 'kind' is simply that of 'minor poetry' and allows a freedom impossible in most of his other works."[9] It seems to me that in *Muiopotmos* we have an example of Spenser's eclectic use of several conventions, and particularly his ability to invent in the manner of the Ovidian metamorphosis and to impress upon conventional elements something of his own style. Lotspeich compares with his success here the Faunus and Molanna interlude in the Mutability Cantos, "in that vein of playful pleasantry, with just a touch of seriousness, which the Elizabethans controlled supremely well."[10]

If *Muiopotmos* offers critical difficulties because of its mixed kind—its opening which promises what the rest of the poem does not precisely perform, and its susceptibility to far-fetched

allegorical interpretations—the poem called *Daphnaida,* dated
January, 1591, offers critical difficulties for almost the opposite
reasons. *Daphnaida* belongs to the love-vision-elegy genre of
which the chief English representative, and Spenser's obvious
model, is Chaucer's *Book of the Duchess. Daphnaida* is organized
with the utmost concern for structure, and there is no apparent
contradiction between the poem's expressed intention and its
performance. Finally, there is no difficulty about explaining the
factual background of the poem; Spenser does some of it himself, and what he failed to do Professor Helen Sandison has
amply done for us.[11] We know that the poem celebrates the sorrow of the poet Sir Arthur Gorges at the death of his young
wife Douglas Howard. Spenser refers to them, under the names
Alcyon and Daphne, in his *Colin Clouts Come Home Againe:*

> And there is sad Alcyon, bent to mourne
> Though fit to frame an euerlasting dittie,
> Whose gentle spright for Daphnes death doth tourn
> Sweet layes of loue to endlesse plaints of pittie.

There is no argument about the interpretation of the poem.

But there is argument about its quality. The Victorian view,
well expressed by Palgrave, found fault with the convention.
This convention of the love-complaint, he said, "seems inevitably
to carry with it no slight obstacles to two elements which poetry can hardly dispense with—contrast and sincerity. And the
sense of this latter deficiency is intensified by the pastoral form
here used without any specific appropriateness, and prolonged
through more than eighty stanzas."[12] Others have complained
that the poem is too long, but it is hard to say what is a proper

CONVENTIONS IN THE MINOR POEMS

length for "the heaviest plaint that ever I heard sound," as
Spenser calls it. He seems to have answered the question arbi-
trarily and artificially by deciding upon seven groups of seven
stanzas (each, of course, seven lines long).

A more general attack upon the poem is that made by C. S.
Lewis in his volume in the *Oxford History of English Literature*.[13] The *Daphnaida* is, he says, "regrettable," "unfortunate"
and "elaborately ugly." "It is a great, flamboyant, garish thing of
stucco disguised as marble," he goes on. "There are, to be sure,
good lines and good images, but it is radically vulgar." . . . [It]
really brings to light an aspect of what I have called the New
Ignorance, for its immense inferiority to the *Duchesse* (itself by
no means one of Chaucer's best works) is not an inferiority of
technique, but of what we should now call civilization; what
the medieval poets themselves would have called *freedom, gen-
tilesse,* and *mesure*." The fault, he thinks, lies chiefly with the
age. "Spenser (like Sidney and Shakespeare) spent most of his
career resisting and curing the new vulgarity. But on this occasion it conquered him."

It may be that *Daphnaida* is as bad as all this when judged by
medieval standards. But I should think an evaluation of it ought
to be preceded by some consideration of what Spenser was trying
to do, and this involves looking backward from the *Daphnaida*
to an earlier poem in praise of a dead lady. The elegy on Dido
in the November eclogue of *The Shepheardes Calender* is a conventional pastoral elegy: various mythical and real personages
are called upon to mourn; the effects upon the shepherds' simple
life are described, and the tone changes toward the end from
grief to consolation. Spenser is imitating Marot, but as E.K. says,

his version passes the reach of the French poet and, indeed, all
the other eclogues in the *Calender*. Spenser converts the conventional complaint into true lyric, as in the stanza

> Whence is it, that the flouret of the field doth fade
> And lyeth buryed long in Winters bale:
> Yet soone as spring his mantle hath displayd,
> It floureth fresh, as it should never fayle?
> But thing on earth that is of most availe,
>> As vertues braunch and beauties budde,
>> Reliuen not for any good.
>>> O heauie herse,
> The braunch once dead, the budde eke needes must
> quaile,
>>> O carefull verse.   (ll. 84–93)

When Spenser came to write the elegy on Douglas Howard
eleven years later he had not only the deceased to celebrate but
her bereaved husband, so the model of Chaucer's *Book of the
Duchess* was the obvious one to follow. In the 1561 edition of
Chaucer which Spenser probably read, the *Book of the Duchess*
is called *Chaucer's Dream;* furthermore, the volume contains
another poem called *The Complaint of the Black Knight,* there
attributed to Chaucer but now known to be by Lydgate. Chaucer
had combined the traditional love-vision with an elegy, and
critical praise of the poem depends upon the skill with which
he combined the two. Spenser in his turn was as much of an
innovator as Chaucer.

In the *Book of the Duchess* Chaucer expends 444 lines before he gets to his mourner, the man in black; most of this is taken up with the usual love-vision machinery of the poet's insomnia, his reading a book, and finally telling the story that he read in the book—in this case the legend of Ceyx and Alcyone. Spenser discards all this as irrelevant, except that he takes the name Alcyon for his mourner. Besides making a much more direct approach than Chaucer, Spenser departs from his convention in another important way. In Chaucer the complaints of the man in black come first, and it is only after some 850 lines of wailing that the cause of the knight's sorrow is revealed. Spenser makes the revelation of the cause a dramatic matter, and the formal complaints follow. First Alcyon tells the news allegorically, in the story of the capture, taming, and loss of a young white lioness, but when the poet does not understand he tells him in direct terms of Daphne's death. Then follows the set of seven plaints, each of seven stanzas seven lines in length. As in the November elegy on Dido, Spenser uses a refrain line to heighten the lyrical effect, "Weep, shepherd, weep, to make my undersong." Spenser blends into these formal complaints much on his favorite themes of mutability and despair; he keeps the structure of the whole thing very formal. But, curiously enough, he succeeds in producing a sense of aesthetic distance and in giving a distinctive flash of himself in the poem when he makes Alcyon say

> Ne let *Elisa* royall Shepheardesse
> The praises of my parted loue enuy,
> For she hath praises in all plenteousnesse,
> Powr'd vpon her, like showers of *Castaly*
> By her owne Shepheard, *Colin* her own Shepherd

That her with heauenly hymnes doth deifie,
Of rusticke muse full hardly to be betterd.

(ll. 225–231)

The older critics, of whom I chose Palgrave as an example, disparaged the poem for lacking what they called contrast and sincerity. I take it that there is ample contrast in the poem if we regard it in the light of its convention. As for sincerity, that is usually an anachronistic concept when applied to Elizabethan poetry. But it happens that the real Alcyon, Sir Arthur Gorges, was a poet too. How did he feel about the lines Spenser provided for him in *Daphnaida* to express his grief? He apparently memorized them (Professor Sandison comments, "as well he might"),[14] for twenty years later, when he was writing a poem on the death of Prince Henry, some of the lines he put down were lines composed by Spenser for Alcyon.

Spenser's *Epithalamion,* some four years later in date than *Daphnaida,* is a poem which needs no defense. It is universally admired, and many readers would agree with DeSelincourt that it is the height of Spenser's poetic achievement. It is also, let us mark, at once the most strictly conventional of all the poems of Spenser and the most personal.

Before we consider the conventional elements in *Epithalamion* and Spenser's method of handling them, it is necessary to return to one of the eclogues in *The Shepheardes Calender* which is in some ways a preliminary exercise for it, as the Dido elegy was for the *Daphnaida.* I mean of course the April eclogue, with its pastoral blazon of Eliza, Queen of Shepherds all. Spenser had already met the problem of form, both structure and versification, in the lyric in praise of Eliza. Furthermore, he had felt his way toward a solution of the difficult artistic problem of the mingling of tones. The lyric is a "silver song," but it must be kept also within the rustic context of pastoral:

> Ye shepheards daughters, that dwell on the greene,
>   hye you there apace:
> Let none come there, but that Virgins bene,
>   to adorne her grace.
> And when you come, whereas shee is in place,
> See, that your rudenesse doe not you disgrace:
>   Binde your fillets faste,
>   And gird in your waste,
> For more finesse, with a tawdrie lace.   (ll. 127–135)

Other preliminary sketches for the *Epithalamion* appear in Book 1 of *The Faerie Queene*. One of them comes in a rather surprising place, the episode of the tempting of Redcrosse by the false Una:

> And she herselfe of beautie soueraigne Queene
> Faire Venus seemde vnto his bed to bring
> Her whom he waking euermore did weene
> To be the chastest flowre, that ay did spring
> On earthly braunch, the daughter of a king,
> Now a loose Leman to vile seruice bound:
> And eke the Graces seemed all to sing,
> Hymen io Hymen, dauncing all around,
> While freshest Flora her with Yuie girlond crownd.
>   (1.i.48)

Another, more obvious and appropriate, is the passage describing the marriage of Una and the Redcrosse Knight at the end of Book 1. Some of the sonnets in *Amoretti* seem to exhibit motifs which Spenser was to use in the *Epithalamion,* particularly Sonnet 15, a blazon which begins "Ye tradefull merchants that with weary toile," and Sonnet 70, an aubade beginning "Fresh spring, the herald of loues mighty king."

Fortunately we have a recent and excellent study of Spenser's use of the conventions in the *Epithalamion,* Thomas M. Greene's essay published in 1957.[15] In Mr. Greene's view, a convention may be regarded as a set of allusions. "A convention exists when the full literary meaning of a word or a line requires a knowledge of many past works in order to be wholly understood. . . . It follows that the first example one encounters in a convention cannot be read as the poet expected his work to be read." The convention of the epithalamion stretches back to Sappho, but its most influential monuments are three poems by Catullus, especially his No. 61. The form was practised by neo-Latin poets of various nationalities, and by French poets of the Pléiade. The only significant examples before Spenser are Sidney's song of the shepherd Dicus at the marriage of Thyrsis and Kala in the *Arcadia*[16] and Bartholomew Young's poem in his translation of Gil Porto's continuation of Montemayor's *Diana.*[17] But there are many after Spenser, by such poets as Chapman, Ben Jonson, Donne, and Herrick, to mention only the most prominent.

In two respects the first English composers of the epithalamion, Sidney, Young, and Spenser, tend to depart from the classical tradition. First, the epithalamion was traditionally an aristocratic poem, celebrating the nuptials of some noble pair; the poet accordingly made his encomia as grossly flattering as poems to the eminent usually were. Sidney's and Young's poems are both pastoral, and Spenser's is bourgeois. Second, the English epithalamion tended to favor a refrain or chorus line, which the classical epithalamion did not do except in the hymn to Hymen. As we have already seen in the *Daphnaida,* Spenser favored a refrain line anyway, so we do not have to attribute the repeated "That all the woods may answer and their echo ring" to the influence of his English predecessors.

One can see in his earlier practice also, particularly in the November and April eclogues of *The Shepheardes Calender,* how natural it was for Spenser to develop an elaborate and highly musical stanza for his verse form. He took some hints from the Italian *canzone* for the *Epithalamion* stanza, but he is far more inventive and experimental than he is imitative in his verse form.

Mr. Greene points out that Spenser departed from convention in two ways other than the social class of the participants and the versification. He fused the figures of the poet and the bridegroom when he wrote an epithalamion for his own wedding. This had consequences with respect to what he could do at the climax and at the end. Furthermore, he introduced some humor, which was made possible by the change of social milieu.

It seems to me that Spenser, while respecting and following the traditions of the classical epithalamion, and expecting of course that learned readers would recognize the allusions and applaud his graceful mastery of them, also took pains to make the poem as native, immediate, and personal as he could, within the limits of decorum. In the first stanza, a traditional invocation of the Muses, he reminds the reader that he is the poet of the *Tears of the Muses* in the volume called *Complaints*. In the fourth stanza he reminds the reader that he lives in Ireland and has a personal pride in the details of his own geographical environment:

> Ye nymphs of Mulla which with carefull heed
> The siluer scaly trouts doe tend full well,
> And greedy pikes which vse therein to feed
> (Those trouts and pikes all others doo excell)
> And ye likewise which keepe the rushy lake,
> Where none doo fishes take . . .   (ll. 56–61)

It is a realistic picture, presented insistently in the foreground against a perspective of Roman deities, traditional symbolic figures, and the whole evocative tradition of the wedding song. The merchant's daughters, the young men of the town who ring the bells, the boys who run up and down the street—they all seem like figures from actual contemporary life. Yet the boys shout, as if they were the creatures of Catullus, "Hymen io Hymen."

The imagery of the description of the bride is emblematic, as it is so often in the *Amoretti;* Spenser is here strongly influenced by the Song of Songs,[18] which he must have considered an epithalamion;

> Her lips lyke cherryes charming men to byte,
> Her brest like to a bowle of cream vncrudded,
> Her paps lyke lyllies budded,
> Her snowie necke lyke to a marble towre,
> And all her body like a pallace fayre,

> Ascending vppe with many a stately stayre,
> To honors seat and chastities sweet bowre.
>
> (ll. 174–180)

Yet in contrast to this highly stylized poetry we have the semi-comic catalogue of night noises:

> Let not the shriech Oule, nor the Storke be heard:
> Nor the night Rauen that still deadly yels,
> Nor damned ghosts cald vp with mighty spels,
> Nor griesly vultures make vs once affeard:
> Ne let the unpleasant Quyre of Frogs still croking
> Make vs to wish theyr choking.
> Let none of these theyr drery accents sing;
> Ne let the woods them answer, nor theyr eccho ring.
>
> (ll. 345–352)

I think Mr. Greene is right in seeing more structure in the poem than the commentators usually do. If the first stanza, the invocation, is considered prefatory, the rest of the poem consists of two 10-stanza sections on each side of the two central stanzas about the church ceremony itself. Then each of the 10-stanza sections is divided into units of 3-4-3. This is an architectural scheme, not found in the conventional epithalamion, but very characteristic of Spenser (recall the seven sevens of seven in *Daphnaida*). He finally addresses his poem:

> Be unto her a goodly ornament
> And for short time an endlesse moniment.

Such design, he felt, was suitable for a poem which was to be ornament and monument. If this strictness of design seem too

stiff or too pedantic for modern readers, perhaps the dazzling
and varied musical qualities of the poem will provide compen-
sation. The music is possible because the convention Spenser was
following took care of many problems and left him free for
song.

Prothalamion is even more completely lyric than the *Epithalamion*. It is a spousal or betrothal song for the two daughters
of the Earl of Worcester; its date in the autumn of 1596 may
thus be established with some exactness. The name *Prothalamion*
seems to be a coinage of Spenser's. No other Elizabethan uses it
except Drayton, who was clearly influenced by Spenser. There
was, however, a convention of such poems. Dan Norton,[19] who
has traced the tradition most fully, shows that betrothal cere-
monies, in life and in fiction, encouraged the composition of
poems, but that the authors of them derived their motifs largely
from the convention of the epithalamion.

Spenser, however, makes use of another tradition—one in
which he himself had already experimented. It is the tradition
of river poems. Sixteen years before the *Prothalamion* Spenser
had composed, in Latin, a poem called *Epithalamion Thamensis*.
It was never published and is now unknown, but one can guess
what it was like from other examples of the genre. Later on,
Spenser composed an elaborate account of the marriage of the
Thames and the Medway for the eleventh canto of Book iv of
The Faerie Queene. And in the very personal and topical poem
Colin Clouts Come Home Againe (1591) he inserted a passage
of 55 lines describing the marriage of two Irish rivers. As worked
out by Osgood forty years ago,[20] the principal themes or motifs
of river poems, as practised by Camden, Leland, Vallans, and

Spenser, were three: (1) a journey of some swans, (2) a marriage of two rivers, and (3) some topographic, antiquarian review of places on the banks of the two rivers.

The obvious qualities of such a poem are learning, especially of an antiquarian sort, facility at mythical invention or adaptation, and copiousness of description. It is the kind of thing for which the talents of Michael Drayton later turned out to be appropriate.

Spenser, in writing the *Prothalamion,* modified the convention in two ways: he returned, as he was so prone to do, to Chaucer and introduced some elements of the dream vision and complaint. The poet opens with a description of the calm, pleasant day, which contrasts with his own mood of "sullein care, / Through discontent of my long fruitlesse stay / In prince's court, and expectation vayne / Of idle hopes, which still do fly away." He sees the water-nymphs gathering flowers; two beautiful swans appear, and the nymphs strew flowers before them and one of them sings a congratulatory lay. Then he reverts to his personal associations by mentioning London as his birthplace, his "most kindly nurse," and recalling that at Essex House, formerly the palace of his patron Leicester, "Oft I gayned giftes and goodly grace / Of that great lord, which therein wont to dwell, / Whose want too well now feedes my freendles case."

The other modification is to extend the allusiveness of the poem not into antiquarian or topographical lore, but to lively current matters of interest. There are puns on the names of Somerset and Devereux. The studious lawyers who now inhabit the Temple are mentioned as well as the ancient Knights Templar. A whole stanza is devoted to the Earl of Essex,

> Great Englands glory and the Worlds wide wonder,
> Whose dreadfull name, late through all Spaine did
>   thunder,
> And Hercules two pillors standing neere,
> Did make to quake and feare.   (ll. 145–149)

The rather cold conventional elements of the river song have
been relieved by the reflective, somewhat melancholy tone of the
poet—a tone which contrasts with the happiness of the occasion.
As he says,

> But Ah here fits not well
> Olde woes but ioyes to tell
> Against the bridale daye, which is not long:
>   Sweet *Themmes* runne softly, till I end my Song.

Furthermore, the journalistic allusiveness of the poem balances
the artifice of the nymphs and the symbolic swans.

No novelties of structure mark the *Prothalamion;* it is less
formal than the *Epithalamion,* and, perhaps for that reason, only
half as long. The movement of the stanzas has been much admired, and the versification in general, as well as Spenser's deft-
ness in manipulating the stanza toward the refrain. That refrain has paid the price of its popularity by serving as ironic contrast in that other poem which uses events on the Thames as
reflections of the values of contemporary life. I mean of course
The Waste Land.

If we try to generalize about Spenser's use of conventions in
the minor poems I think we must make at least the following
observations. Spenser was a poet to whom the conventions were
still alive. He saw them used by contemporary French and Italian

writers as well as by the ancients. In fact, I do not think that he felt there was as much chronological difference between the ancients and the moderns as do we. In some sense Eliot's famous remark can be applied to Spenser, that for him the whole of European literature from Homer to the present day had a contemporaneous existence.

To be sure, Spenser adapted the conventions to his own use. In doing this he was following in the footsteps of his master Chaucer and showing the way to his disciple Milton. Like them he felt that the personal element in poetry, the reflection of the mind and temper of the individual writer, is expressed most vividly when it is embedded in a convention. Like them also, he saw to it that his work was distinctively English, that it displayed an instinctive and intimate love of English rivers and flowers and trees, and an artist's pride in the English language.

LOUIS L. MARTZ

The *Amoretti:* "Most Goodly Temperature"

MOST OF US, I imagine, have at one time or another felt some degree of disappointment in reading Spenser's *Amoretti*. These sonnets have often seemed rather tame and flat when compared with Sidney's or with Shakespeare's, or even with Drayton's best: our sage and serious Spenser, perhaps, lacked the wit and compression necessary for distinguished work within the sonnet medium; his melody, his craft, his emblematic techniques, his strong idealism may not be adequate to lift the *Amoretti* very far above their heavy reliance on the Petrarchan conventions.

At the same time we may tend to agree with the argument strongly advanced by J. W. Lever in one of the most recent, and one of the best, interpretations of the *Amoretti:* that the sonnets show irreconcilable inconsistencies in the presentation of the heroine. In most of the poems we find a "lofty conception" of the lady as angelic, divine, purely virtuous; and yet in many others she is represented as cruel, murderous, savage, guileful, tormenting. As a result, Mr. Lever finds here "an attempted blending of two collections of sonnets, differing in subject-matter, characterization, and general conception." He believes that we can best deal with the sequence "by setting apart those sonnets which evidently belong to an earlier phase and run counter to the general stream of thought and feeling"; he singles out "at least some eighteen sonnets best considered apart from the main group"—all of them relating to the cruel "Tyrannesse." [1]

Moreover, it has sometimes been charged that the series is lacking in proportion: the change in the lover's mood occurs too quickly at the second New Year, and the happy sonnets that follow are outweighed by the mass of earlier complaints. And finally, we have the problems raised by the ending of the sequence, which many readers have found abrupt and disconcerting, as the mood suddenly turns from contentment to distress, in the last four sonnets, and we are left with the puzzling group of anacreontic verses between us and the great *Epithalamion*.

All these objections are so closely related that to deal with one is to deal with all. Let me start with the last. A careful study of the opening sonnet will be of great help here, for Sonnet 1, as prologue and dedication to the whole, seems to link directly with the last three sonnets and to give us both the physical and the emotional setting in which all the sonnets should be read. The poet first addresses those happy leaves of paper which are about to receive his lady's touch:

> Happy ye leaues when as those lilly hands,
> > which hold my life in their dead doing might
> shall handle you and hold in loues soft bands,
> lyke captiues trembling at the victors sight.

and hold in loues soft bands: the phrase implies more than her physical touch; the poet seems assured that his poems will be welcomed and cherished by her love. He does not need to beg her to read them; he knows that she will read them:

And happy lines, on which with starry light,
   those lamping eyes will deigne sometimes to look
and reade the sorrowes of my dying spright,
   written with teares in harts close bleeding book.
And happy rymes bath'd in the sacred brooke,
   of *Helicon* whence she deriued is,
when ye behold that Angels blessed looke,
   my soules long lacked foode, my heauens blis.

my soules long lacked foode: he has been absent from her "blessed
looke" for a long while, it seems, and these poems are now being
sent off to her, a record of the whole courtship up to this point
of their separation. But the poet does not endure this separation
in doubt and anguish. He is writing now from a standpoint in
which he can review his sorrows with the calm assurance of a
mutual affection, an assurance, a poise, a security of mind represented in this poem's highly symmetrical construction. "Happy
ye leaues . . . / And happy lines . . . / And happy rymes";
and then the final couplet, binding all together:

   Leaues, lines, and rymes, seeke her to please alone,
     whom if ye please, I care for other none.

All this seems to point toward the situation, mood, and tone of
the last three sonnets (87, 88, 89), unless we choose to read them
in an unjustified relation to Sonnet 86, where the poet tells how
a "Venemous toung," "with false forged lyes," "in my true loue
did stirre vp coles of yre." But the ending of this sonnet may be
taken to suggest the failure of the slanderer[2]

         that didst with guile conspire
   in my sweet peace such breaches to haue bred.

And there is no indication in the three following sonnets that
his lady's anger has continued or that these slanders have caused
the separation here recorded. There is no sign that he is in dis-
grace, that he is barred from her presence by anger and disdain.
He has simply left the presence of his love and he now spends the
time "with expectation," in a state of mind that "maketh euery
minute seeme a myle" (Sonnet 87). For all we know, the separation may have been caused by preparations for their wedding.
All we know is that, for a time, he has "lackt the comfort of
that light" that radiates from his lady's presence, and must main-
tain himself by "beholding the Idaea" of her radiance:

> with light thereof I doe my selfe sustayne,
> and thereon feed my loue-affamisht hart.   (Sonnet 88)

The situation, then, seems to be much the same as that implied
by "my soules long lacked foode" in Sonnet 1. Finally, the series
comes to rest in Sonnet 89, where the lover's sorrow is presented
as deriving from the temporary separation of two assured mates:

> Lyke as the Culuer on the bared bough,
>> Sits mourning for the absence of her mate:
>> and in her songs sends many a wishfull vow,
>> for his returne that seemes to linger late.
> So I alone now left disconsolate,
>> mourne to my selfe the absence of my loue:
>> and wandring here and there all desolate,
>> seek with my playnts to match that mournful doue:
> Ne ioy of ought that vnder heauen doth houe,
>> can comfort me, but her owne ioyous sight:
>> whose sweet aspect both God and man can moue,

in her vnspotted pleasauns to delight.
Dark is my day, whyles her fayre light I mis,
and dead my life that wants such liuely blis.

The most appropriate sequel to such a mood of "expectation"
is the joyful *Epithalamion* that Spenser has given us; I do not feel
the abruptness and uncertainty that some have found in the
conclusion of the *Amoretti*. One touch of slander cannot spoil
this kind of love; and indeed Sonnet 86 presents only one of
several futile threats to the lovers' security which Spenser deals
with toward the end of his sequence. Separation is one threat,
which the whole sequence strives to overcome. The envy of the
world, in Sonnet 85, is another threat, coming from those witless
cuckoos who "when I doe praise her, say I doe but flatter." His
recurrent sense of his own unworthiness, in Sonnet 82, is
still another. Sonnets 83 and 84, if read in a paired relationship,
suggest the discontents arising from his own "hungry eyes" and
"greedy couetize"; these unruly tendencies are suppressed, or at
least controlled, in Sonnet 84 by vowing:

Let not one sparke of filthy lustfull fyre
    breake out, that may her sacred peace molest:
    ne one light glance of sensuall desyre
    Attempt to work her gentle mindes vnrest.

Instead, he will attempt to convert such rude emotions into
"pure affections" and "modest thoughts"; and he concludes,
rather ruefully,

but speake no word to her of these sad plights,
    which her too constant stiffenesse doth constrayn.

Onely behold her rare perfection,
     and blesse your fortunes fayre election.

Sonnet 83, of course, is the notorious repetition of Sonnet 35;
this repetition has been taken as evidence that the sequence was
hastily gathered together, and therefore as a justification for
questioning the contents and arrangement of the first edition,
our only authority. It is certainly possible that Spenser simply
forgot to cross out the sonnet in one place after changing its
position and revising one word. On the other hand, the sonnet
is appropriate in either place, and its double occurrence might
be taken, not as a slip, but as a reprise: a designed reminiscence
and recurrence of an earlier mood of pining and complaint.

In any case, these varied threats to contentment seem entirely
appropriate after the long rich climax of almost unalloyed happiness that has run from Sonnet 63, where he at last descries
"the happy shore," down through the culmination of her praise
in Sonnet 81, with its balanced, symmetrical blazon of his lady's
beauty, both in body and in spirit:

Fayre is my loue, when her fayre golden heares,
     with the loose wynd ye wauing chance to marke:
fayre when the rose in her red cheekes appeares,
     or in her eyes the fyre of loue does sparke.
Fayre when her brest lyke a rich laden barke,
     with pretious merchandize she forth doth lay:
fayre when that cloud of pryde, which oft doth dark
     her goodly light with smiles she driues away.
But fayrest she, when so she doth display
     the gate with pearles and rubyes richly dight:

> throgh which her words so wise do make their way
> to beare the message of her gentle spright.
> The rest be works of natures wonderment,
> but this the worke of harts astonishment.

The only qualifications to his happiness here are slight, and very easily overcome: her fear of losing her liberty (Sonnet 65); a suggestion that he is too "meane a one" for her (Sonnet 66); several intimations of mortality (Sonnets 72, 75, 79); and one mild lamentation of her absence (Sonnet 78). Spenser, I think, greatly strengthens the *Amoretti* at the very close by bringing his joy within a harsher context of worldly reality. Their love is not impaired by these threats, but it learns to live within the world, as it must. The great *Epithalamion* then emerges happily out of its own triumphant accommodation with the world. (It will be evident that I have only one solution to offer for the intervening anacreontics: ignore them.)

But what of the other alleged disproportions and inconsistencies in the sequence? These too, I feel, tend to disappear within a dominant tone of assurance and poise and mutual understanding that controls the series. This peculiar and highly original relationship between the lover and his lady may be our best key to the whole sequence. It involves a variety of closely related issues: how does the lover characterize himself? what attitudes does he adopt toward the lady? what sort of audience does she provide? how does she receive his addresses? It is worth while to examine first the nature of this lady, for she talks and acts more than most of these heroines do. Most Petrarchan ladies, as Pope might say, "have no characters at all"; and even Sidney's

Stella, though she comes to display considerable adroitness in damping her lover's ardors, remains for most of the sequence a black-eyed effigy around which Astrophel performs his brilliant Portrait of the Lover as a very young dog.

But Spenser's lady has a very decided and a very attractive character.[3] First of all, it is clear that the lover's tributes to "her mind adornd with vertues manifold" (Sonnet 15), her "deep wit" (Sonnet 43), her "gentle wit, and vertuous mind" (Sonnet 79), her "words so wise," "the message of her gentle spright" (Sonnet 81)—it is clear that all these tributes to her mental powers are very well deserved. Quite early in the sequence, in the paired Sonnets 28 and 29, we find the lady wittily turning the tables on her lover in a dialogue that throws a bright light on their peculiar relationship. In Sonnet 28 the lover has noticed that she is wearing a laurel leaf, and this sign, he says, "giues me great hope of your relenting mynd," since it is the poet's own symbol; he goes on to warn her of the fate that befell proud Daphne when she fled from the god of poetry, and he ends with the witty turn:

> Then fly no more fayre loue from Phebus chace,
>   but in your brest his leafe and loue embrace.

Then in Sonnet 29 the lady pertly carries on this play of wit:

> See how the stubborne damzell doth depraue
>   my simple meaning with disdaynfull scorne:
>   and by the bay which I vnto her gaue,
>   accoumpts my selfe her captiue quite forlorne.
> The bay (quoth she) is of the victours borne,
>   yielded them by the vanquisht as theyr meeds,

> and they therewith doe poetes heads adorne,
> to sing the glory of their famous deedes.

All right, he says, since she claims the conquest, "let her accept me as her faithfull thrall":

> Then would I decke her head with glorious bayes,
> and fill the world with her victorious prayse.

I do not see how this interchange can be taken as anything but smiling and good-humored, yes, even humorous, in our sense of the word. The phrase "stubborne damzell" tells us a great deal about the poet's tone here: it is intimate, smiling, affectionate, respectful, reproachful, and courtly, all at once: it strikes exactly the tone that an older man, of experience and wisdom (someone a bit like Emma's Mr. Knightley) might adopt toward a bright and beautiful and willful young lady for whom he feels, not awe, but deep admiration and affection. It is an attitude that also implies considerable hope and confidence that his suit will in time be rewarded. It is an attitude that finds a fulfillment and perfect counterpart later on, after his acceptance, in the gentle wit of Sonnet 71, which even Mr. Lever takes as "affectionate banter" (p. 130). This is the sonnet where the lady, in a witty reversal of the poet's complaints, has woven into her embroidery a fable of the Bee and the Spyder; the poet picks up the imagery with joy and develops it with a deeply affectionate humor. Indeed, throughout the sequence she is certainly one of the most smiling and "chearefull" ladies to appear in any English sequence, and I doubt that her smiles are outdone anywhere on the Continent. Sonnets 39 and 40, wholly devoted to her smiling and her "amiable cheare," are only the most sustained of many indications of her

"sweet eye-glaunces" and her "charming smiles" (Sonnet 17).
In view of this it is hard to see why readers have insisted upon
taking the whole sequence so solemnly. Sonnet 16, very early in
the game, is enough in itself to tell us otherwise, with its playful,
deliberately hyperbolic, and clearly smiling use of the Alexandrian
Cupid:

> One day as I vnwarily did gaze
>> on those fayre eyes my loues immortall light:
>> the whiles my stonisht hart stood in amaze,
>> through sweet illusion of her lookes delight;
> I mote perceiue how in her glauncing sight,
>> legions of loues with little wings did fly:
>> darting their deadly arrowes fyry bright,
>> at euery rash beholder passing by.
> One of those archers closely I did spy,
>> ayming his arrow at my very hart:
>> when suddenly with twincle of her eye,
>> the Damzell broke his misintended dart.
> Had she not so doon, sure I had bene slayne,
>> yet as it was, I hardly scap't with paine.

Now the meaning of "twincle" as a wink, a nod, a hint, was current in Elizabethan usage; a damsel with a twinkle would seem
to hold here every modern connotation. At the same time, the
strong colloquialism of the last two lines seems to warn us with
a similar twinkle not to take this lover's professions of grief too
solemnly.

But what then shall we make of Mr. Lever's eighteen excom-
municated sonnets, along with others of this kind, where the

lady commits those "huge massacres" with her eyes, and as a "cruell warriour"

> greedily her fell intent poursewth,
> Of my poore life to make vnpittied spoile.
>
> (Sonnet 11)

Many of these are done with such extravagant exaggeration of the conventional poses that they strike me as close to mock-heroic. These are the conventions of love, the poet seems to say; these are the usual rituals of courtship; he will gladly pay these tributes, and even overpay them, since this is what his delightful damsel seems to expect, and she thoroughly deserves this state; at the same time a girl of her deep wit will know exactly how to take them, in the spirit offered. She can be expected to respond with a smile and a witty rejoinder, as she does in Sonnet 18, herself outdoing the Petrarchan poses:

> But when I pleade, she bids me play my part,
>   and when I weep, she sayes teares are but water:
>   and when I sigh, she sayes I know the art,
>   and when I waile, she turnes hir selfe to laughter.

We can begin to see, then, the kind of relationship in which these charges of cruelty are uttered; we can begin to anticipate the sort of tone that the lover will tend to adopt in paying his conventional tributes.

Spenser's title is in itself a clue: *Amoretti,* the diminutive form, implying a relationship of intimate affection; it might be translated as: "intimate little tokens of love." [4] At the same time, the Italian title seems to draw a special attention to the great Continental tradition from which the sequence takes its themes, its imagery, its form. A complete definition might read: *Amoretti*, "intimate little tokens of love made out of ancient materials deriving, primarily, from Italy."

And so we have:

> Vnrighteous Lord of loue what law is this,
>   That me thou makest thus tormented be?
>   the whiles she lordeth in licentious blisse
>   of her freewill, scorning both thee and me.
> See how the Tyrannesse doth ioy to see
>   the huge massacres which her eyes do make:
>   and humbled harts brings captiues vnto thee,
>   that thou of them mayst mightie vengeance take.
> But her proud hart doe thou a little shake
>   and that high look, with which she doth comptroll
>   all this worlds pride bow to a baser make,
>   and al her faults in thy black booke enroll.
> That I may laugh at her in equall sort,
>   as she doth laugh at me and makes my pain her sport.
>
> (Sonnet 10)

The tone here is very hard to describe. It would be too much to call it parody, and yet the postures seem to be deliberately judged by the presence of some degree of smiling. It would be too much to call the sonnet comic, and yet, if we temper the term rightly, there is an element of comedy here, though not so broad as in the sonnet with the "twincle." At the same time, of course, a great many of these sonnets of complaint are delivered in a straightforward manner, and others allow little more than the glimmer of a smile to break through in the last line or two. I am arguing only that the series is frequently touched with an element that we might call humor, parody, or comedy; it is a light touch, but it is, I think, sovereign. Among the sixty sonnets that come within the first year of courtship, it is possible to single out at least fifteen that seem clearly to display this transforming humor (for example: Sonnets 10, 12, 16, 18, 20, 24, 26, 28, 29, 30, 32, 33, 37, 43, 46, 48, 50, 57); and their presence is bound to have considerable effect upon our reading of all the other sonnets of complaint. As prime examples I would instance Sonnet 30, where Spenser drives into absurdity the old Petrarchan cliché: "My loue is lyke to yse, and I to fyre"; or Sonnet 32, where the homely image of the "paynefull smith" beating the iron with "his heauy sledge" prepares the way for an account of how the lover's "playnts and prayers" beat futilely "on th' anduyle of her stubberne wit";

> What then remaines but I to ashes burne,
>   and she to stones at length all frosen turne?

Lines such as these, so close to parody, need not be taken as utterly inconsistent with those other sonnets, such as 7, 8, and 9, where the poet praises his lady's angelic virtue, with that famous tribute to her eyes:

> Then to the Maker selfe they likest be,
>   whose light doth lighten all that here we see.
>   (Sonnet 9)

Does the opening line of the next sonnet (10)—"Vnrighteous Lord of loue what law is this, / That me thou makest thus tormented be?"—conflict with that exalted view of the lady? On

the contrary, the poet seems to be making a clear distinction between those essential qualities deriving from the heavenly Maker,
and those "cruelties" demanded by conventional Cupid, the un-
righteous Lord of love, the adversary of the "glorious Lord of
lyfe" who in Sonnet 68 teaches the lovers their devout lesson of
love.

These two aspects of the lady's portrait (essence and appearance) are frequently considered together in the same sonnet,
where their incongruity is fully recognized, as in Sonnet 31,
which concludes:

> But did she know how ill these two accord,
>   such cruelty she would have soone abhord.

Or again, in Sonnet 24, we find the same awareness of this
contradiction, in a mode closer to the comic:

> When I behold that beauties wonderment,
>   And rare perfection of each goodly part:
>   of natures skill the onely complement,
>   I honor and admire the makers art.
> But when I feele the bitter balefull smart,
>   which her fayre eyes vnwares doe worke in mee:
>   that death out of theyr shiny beames doe dart,
>   I thinke that I a new *Pandora* see. . . .

But it all ends with a playful suggestion:

> But since ye are my scourge I will intreat,
>   that for my faults ye will me gently beat.

Likewise in Sonnet 26 we have that witty series of playful ep-
igrams, all stressing his lady's double aspect:

Sweet is the Rose, but growes vpon a brere;
  Sweet is the Iunipere, but sharpe his bough;
  sweet is the Eglantine, but pricketh nere;
  sweet is the firbloome, but his braunches rough.
Sweet is the Cypresse, but his rynd is tough,
  sweet is the nut, but bitter is his pill;
  sweet is the broome-flowre, but yet sowre enough;
  and sweet is Moly, but his root is ill.
So euery sweet with soure is tempred still,
  that maketh it be coueted the more:

And in Sonnet 45 we have, fully developed, the view that her
essential being is belied by her proud and tyrannic aspects; here
the lover, with a tone of excessive courtesy, urges the lady to
stop looking in her mirror, "Your goodly selfe for euermore to
vew," and instead to seek within her lover's "inward selfe" the
image of her "semblant trew":

Within my hart, though hardly it can shew
  thing so diuine to vew of earthly eye:
  the fayre Idea of your celestiall hew,
  and euery part remaines immortally:
And were it not that through your cruelty,
  with sorrow dimmed and deformd it were:
  the goodly ymage of your visnomy,
  clearer then christall would therein appere.
But if your selfe in me ye playne will see,
  remoue the cause by which your fayre
  beames darkned be.

In still other sonnets the lover attempts to make a virtue of
necessity by converting her twofold aspect into an example of

"most goodly temperature": "Myld humblesse mixt with awfull
maiesty" (Sonnet 13):

> Was it the worke of nature or of Art,
>   which tempred so the feature of her face,
>   that pride and meeknesse mixt by equall part,
>   doe both appeare t'adorne her beauties grace?
>
> (Sonnet 21)

In short, the sonnets that deal with the proud and cruel fair
form an indispensable part of the series; they represent the due
and proper acknowledgment of all the usual forms of tribute:

> Bring therefore all the forces that ye may,
>   and lay incessant battery to her heart,
>   playnts, prayers, vowes, ruth, sorrow, and dismay,
>   those engins can the proudest loue conuert.
> And if those fayle fall downe and dy before her,
>   so dying liue, and liuing do adore her.

Sonnet 14 thus foretells the use of every possible mode of Petrarchan approach, and the series thoroughly fulfills the promise, in
many various modes: exalted, solemn, tender, touched with the
edge of a smile, tinged with a hint of wit, or broadly comic.

Then, as we come close to the point where the lover discovers
his acceptance, we find the rich variety of all the earlier sonnets
summed up for us in Sonnet 54, which is perhaps more important
than any other individual sonnet for an understanding of the
sequence:

> Of this worlds Theatre in which we stay,
>   My loue lyke the Spectator ydly sits
>   beholding me that all the pageants play,

> disguysing diuersly my troubled wits.
> Sometimes I ioy when glad occasion fits,
> and mask in myrth lyke to a Comedy:
> soone after when my ioy to sorrow flits,
> I waile and make my woes a Tragedy.

Those lines provide the best possible answer to any who might doubt the presence of mirth and comedy in the sequence; but more important is the way in which this sonnet indicates the complete recognition of the lover that he is deliberately playing many parts, staging "all the pageants" in an ancient festival of courtship, adopting all the masks that may catch his lady's eye and prove his devotion.

> Yet she beholding me with constant eye,
> delights not in my merth nor rues my smart:
> but when I laugh she mocks, and when I cry
> she laughes, and hardens euermore her hart.
> What then can moue her? if nor merth nor mone,
> she is no woman, but a sencelesse stone.

But actually these pageants have achieved their end; the festival of courtship is nearly over, and only a few sonnets later (63, 64) the lover receives his due acknowledgment from this thoroughly composed and constant young lady. The lover's own assurance that he will soon be openly accepted appears to be suggested just before the end of the year's courtship, in the paired Sonnets 58 and 59, which constitute some kind of dialogue on the lady's self-assurance. Some have thought that the heading of Sonnet 58, "By her that is most assured to her selfe," belongs rather with

Sonnet 59, which may be taken as the lady's reply to the lover's query in the immediately preceding lines:

> Why then doe ye proud fayre, misdeeme so farre,
>   that to your selfe ye most assured arre?

In my original version of this paper I tended to accept this point of view; but William Nelson and Leicester Bradner have convinced me that the word "By" in this heading must be used in the old sense of "concerning," as Gascoigne used it in the headings to several of his poems.[5] Thus the poet has composed a pair of sonnets on this problem: rebuke and palinode; and he has phrased the second in a way that allows it to be taken as a representation of the lady's point of view. She does not misdeem; she knows precisely what she is doing:

> Thrise happie she, that is so well assured
>   Vnto her selfe and setled so in hart:
>   that nether will for better be allured,
>   ne feard with worse to any chaunce to start,
> But like a steddy ship doth strongly part
>   the raging waues and keepes her course aright:
>   ne ought for tempest doth from it depart,
>   ne ought for fayrer weathers false delight.

Here is the sage and serious lady, the poet's proper mate, who in Sonnet 75 so wisely rebukes her lover's efforts to write her name in the sand; but now at the close of Sonnet 59 the sternness changes to a promising smile:

> Most happy she that most assured doth rest,
>   but he most happy who such one loues best.

That compact final line assumes a quiet understanding between this lover and his lady. For how can he be happy who loves such a one, unless she will return his love with all the power of her constancy? In fact, if we allow for a colloquial looseness in the use of relative pronouns, we may find a double meaning in the word "who." He is indeed most happy who such a one loves best.

The next four sonnets, in many ways, represent the full peripeteia of the series. Sonnet 60 formally marks the anniversary of their courtship (something like a "whole years work" has been mentioned in Sonnet 23: we may take the intervening sonnets as a full memorial of that year); and at the same time we are told the lover's age: he is forty. This revelation (which seems to astound and dismay even graduate students) explains a great deal that may have puzzled us about the lover's manner and tone; it confirms our impression that the foregoing sonnets are written from the broad, experienced view of maturity, written with a witty and mature consciousness that has mastered all the modes of courtship. He is in love; he knows his lady's nature; and although he would be grieved if she should reject him, he never really accepts this possibility.

The presence of this assured attitude throughout the series is clearly demonstrated by the two sonnets (33 and 80) in which he alludes to his writing of *The Faerie Queene*. In the first of these he tells his friend Lodwick that he finds it impossible to work upon the poem, for his troubles with his proud lady have completely distracted him:

> How then should I without another wit,
> thinck euer to endure so taedious toyle?

> sins that this one is tost with troublous fit,
> of a proud loue, that doth my spirite spoyle.

Since this comes directly after the witty Sonnet 32, we may well suspect a strong degree of posturing in this boyish excuse; and our suspicion is borne out in Sonnet 80, where it appears that he has in fact been working on the poem all the while; he has completed six books, and he now asks leave to rest at this convenient half-way point, "and gather to my selfe new breath awhile."

> Till then giue leaue to me in pleasant mew,
>   to sport my muse and sing my loues sweet praise:
> the contemplation of whose heauenly hew,
>   my spirit to an higher pitch will rayse.
> But let her prayses yet be low and meane,
>   fit for the handmayd of the Faery Queene.

There is no danger that this discreet lover will ever lose his strong sense of duty and propriety.

This attitude of mature consciousness (or middle-aged discretion, if you will) has been conveyed throughout by the poise and harmony of Spenser's poetical techniques. The steady beat of his intricate rime-scheme is varied only in Sonnet 8, where we may feel that the Shakespearean form serves to stress, by emphatic variation, the goodly temperature that his lady has already begun to develop in this lover:

> You frame my thoughts and fashion me within,
>   you stop my toung, and teach my hart to speake,
> you calme the storme that passion did begin,
>   strong thrugh your cause, but by your vertue weak.

This balance and symmetry of structure, firmly represented in the first sonnet, recurs at frequent intervals throughout the series: Sonnet 56, a lament for her cruelty, displays a structure very similar to that of Sonnet 1; and there are many varieties of such tightly balanced construction, as in the comparisons of Sonnets 9 and 26. Here is another reason why the assertions of his "bitter balefull smart" are taken as a tribute, not as an emotional fact. The statements of his suffering are artifacts presented as adornments, offerings, and "moniments." Meanwhile Spenser's tactful deployment of archaic diction and his frequent reminiscence of the old-fashioned alliterative verse both contribute to the total impression of a lover who has a deep respect and affection for the ancient, traditional, formal modes of utterance.

And now, at the moment of full peripeteia, Sonnet 61 retracts all charges laid against her pride and cruelty, and casts the full weight of the lover's adoration toward the celebration of her divine essence:

> The glorious image of the makers beautie,
>> My souerayne saynt, the Idoll of my thought,
>> dare not henceforth aboue the bounds of dewtie,
>> t'accuse of pride, or rashly blame for ought.
> For being as she is diuinely wrought,
>> and of the brood of Angels heuenly borne:
>> and with the crew of blessed Saynts vpbrought,
>> each of which did her with theyr guifts adorne;
> The bud of ioy, the blossome of the morne,
>> the beame of light, whom mortal eyes admyre:
>> what reason is it then but she should scorne

base things that to her loue too bold aspire?
  Such heauenly formes ought rather worship be,
    then dare be lou'd by men of meane degree.

So then in Sonnet 62 the New Year begins again, "with shew
of morning mylde," "betokening peace and plenty to ensew." This
outer "chaunge of weather," as he suggests, betokens a change of
inner weather, in which both lover and lady cease their pageants
and return each other's love without a mask. In Sonnet 63 he
clearly descries "the happy shore", and in Sonnet 64 the great
sequence of joy is fully launched with his ritual celebration of
their kiss, recalling, as Israel Baroway has pointed out,[6] the
poetical techniques of the Song of Solomon—though we should
add that Spenser gives to these techniques his own witty turns:

Her lips did smell lyke vnto Gillyflowers,
  her ruddy cheekes lyke vnto Roses red:
  her snowy browes lyke budded Bellamoures,
  her louely eyes lyke Pincks but newly spred,
Her goodly bosome lyke a Strawberry bed,
  her neck lyke to a bounch of Cullambynes:
  her brest lyke lillyes, ere theyr leaues be shed,
  her nipples lyke yong blossomd Iessemynes:

So all the modes of being from earth to heaven are now woven
together into a full Spenserian harmony. His love moves to the
steady measure of the calendar, both secular and religious. The
reprise of the New Year's motif, recalling Sonnet 4, and the reprise of the Spring song in Sonnet 70, recalling both Sonnet 4
and Sonnet 19, place the lovers' lives in tune with the seasons of
nature; meanwhile the great Easter sonnet (68), recalling the

"holy season fit to fast and pray" of Sonnet 22, places the whole series in a firm accord with the lessons of the Lord of life. And finally, climax of harmony, we have Sonnet 74, where the unity of life is celebrated through the symbolism of the three Elizabeths: his mother, his queen, and his lady. Only a poet so persistently harmonious as Spenser could have managed to arrange so perfect an accord of filial piety, courtly fealty, and virtuous betrothal.

Most goodly temperature indeed: in that one phrase Spenser has given us the best possible account of the *Amoretti,* as he leads us back to the ancient roots and affiliations of the word *temperature: temperatura, temperatus, temperatio;* signifying, in the terms of my Latin dictionary: a due mingling, fit proportion, proper combination, symmetry, a regulating power, an organizing principle.

Notes

A. C. HAMILTON
The Visions of *Piers Plowman* and *The Faerie Queene*

1. In this paper I have used by permission an article that appeared originally as "Spenser and Langland" in *SP*, LV (1958), 533–48, and occasional phrases from *The Structure of Allegory in The Faerie Queene* (Oxford, 1961).

2. *The Vision of . . . Piers the Plowman,* ed. by Skeat (E.E.T.S., 1869). This edition of the Crowley text is cited throughout.

3. See "The Argument of Spenser's *Shepheardes Calender,*" *ELH,* XXIII (1956), 171–82.

4. *The Vision of Pierce Plowman, nowe the second tyme imprinted* . . . (1550), sig. ii^v.

5. I am indebted to H. W. Wells for pointing out this parallel structure, though my statement differs from his. See his "The Construction of *Piers Plowman,*" *PMLA,* XLIV (1929), 123–40.

6. H. Meroney discusses the threefold scheme of Christian spirituality in Langland. See his "The Life and Death of Longe Wille," *ELH,* XVII (1950), 10–11. J. B. Collins finds Spenser's Canto x to be "an excellent exemplification, in the form of allegory, of the methodology of Christian mysticism." *Christian Mysticism in the Elizabethan Age* (Baltimore, 1940), p. 193.

7. J. Lawlor, " 'Piers Plowman': the Pardon Reconsidered," *MLR,* XLV (1950), 456.

8. Spenser uses the term in the *July* eclogue where the shepherd Thomalin denounces the proud ignorant priest as "a lewde lorrell" (93). I owe this reference to Hebel's edition of *The Works of Michael Drayton* (Oxford, 1941), V.7.

9. John Lawlor, "The Imaginative Unity of *Piers Plowman*," *RES*, VIII (1957), 114.

10. C. H. Herford *et al., Ben Jonson* (Oxford, 1947), VIII, 639.

11. *Wilson's Arte of Rhetorique,* ed. by G. H. Mair (Oxford, 1909), pp. 100, 104.

12. See "A Theological Reading of *The Faerie Queene,* Book II," *ELH,* XXV (1958), 155–62.

13. Wilson, p. 7.

14. Wilson, p. 7. Cf. "There are two parts of a conclusion, the one resteth in gathering together briefly, all such arguments as were before rehearsed [the Palmer's comment upon the end of the intemperate life] . . . the other part of a conclusion, resteth . . . in augmenting and vehemently enlarging that, which before was in fewe wordes spoken [the vehement scorn of Grill]" (p. 114).

15. See " 'Like Race to Runne': the Parallel Structure of *The Faerie Queene,* Books I and II," *PMLA,* LXXIII (1958), 327–34.

16. Cf. Lawlor: "What is central to Langland's whole design is the observed discrepancy between what we believe and what in fact we are. His poem has its focus in this aspect of the human condition" (p. 122).

17. *Convivio,* trans. by W. W. Jackson (Oxford, 1909), p. 74. See his letter to Can Grande in *The Letters of Dante,* trans. by Paget Toynbee (Oxford, 1920). See C. S. Singleton, *Dante Studies, I* (Cambridge, 1957), pp. 84 f.

18. Milton, *Il Penseroso,* ll. 119–20.

19. "An Apology for Poetry," in *Elizabethan Critical Essays,* ed. by G. Gregory Smith (Oxford, 1904), I, 184.

20. "The Pardon of Piers Plowman," *Proceedings of the British Academy,* XXX (1944), 350.

HARRY BERGER, JR.

A Secret Discipline

1. I should like to acknowledge the invaluable help given me by Richard B. Young, with whom many of the general notions in this paper were telephonically worked out on a two-party line.

2. I have discussed this aspect of Book II at length in *The Allegorical Temper* (New Haven, 1957).

3. The Temple of Venus is displayed as the product, the Marriage of Rivers as the embodied process of human imagination. A good epigraph for these cantos may be found in the commonplace from Ovid's *Ars Amatoriae*, ii.401–402:

> Si Venerem Cois nunquam pinxit Apelles
> Mersa sub aequoreis illa lateret aquis.

4. Thus we are left in the air about the future of Tristram, the Noble Savage, and Matilda's child (VI.ii.40, v.1–2, iv.38).

5. VI.viii.17–18, 22, 29–30.

6. At VI.iii.18–19 Calidore leaves Priscilla with her father, and we never find out whether or not she is reunited with her lover Aladine, though this is the main point of the episode. Similarly, the fate of Calidore and Pastorella is ignored (xii.22), though a reader might divine it without the help of the gods. Perhaps the most flagrant example of this motif comes at the end of Canto viii, when Spenser abandons Calepine in the dark with the naked Serena, who nervously waits for daylight to "discover bad and good." The sudden shift from the problems of murder to those of modesty is characteristic of the disequilibrium Spenser maintains in this book. One might ask, incidentally, what the poet had in mind when he picked those good humanist names, Calepine and Aldus.

7. See VI.ii.40; iv.17; v.11; vi.17; vii.27; viii.4, 31, 51; ix.1,46; x.1–3; xi.24; xii.1–2, 14, 22.

8. VI.iv.29–33.

9. vi.iv.16; v.31, 39; vi.1–15.

10. vi.pr.3–4, 7; i.1; iv.11–14; v.1–2; vi.9–12; ix.20; x.22–23. By *nursery* is meant simply the concept of *source* in its various aspects.

11. Examples: vi.i.2; ii.2, 24; iii.1–2; v.1–2; vii.1–2, 28; viii.1–2; ix.20–23.

12. vi.iv.32–38; ix.14; xii.3–9.

13. vi.ii.27–30; v.11–23; v.36–vi.4; ix.24–31; x.2–3, 9, 22; xii.19–21.

14. vi.ii.16–18; iii.20–21, 23–24; iv.17; v.10–11, 15; vii.6–7, 18–19; viii.34; x.18, 34, 39; xii.40–41.

15. vi.iv.14, 23–24, 38; v.10–11, 38; vi.19; vii.24; viii.35; ix.1–xii.4 *passim*.

16. "The Truancy of Calidore," in *That Soueraine Light*, ed. by W. R. Mueller and D. C. Allen (Baltimore, 1952), p. 68.

17. For the double meaning of *blatant*, see Leslie Hotson, "The Blatant Beast," in *Studies in Honor of T. W. Baldwin*, ed. by D. C. Allen (Urbana, 1958), pp. 34–38.

18. In the early version of this paper, "The Prospect of Imagination," *Studies in English Literature*, I (Winter, 1961), 106–7.

19. "Truancy of Calidore," pp. 68–69.

20. *De Amore* II.2–4, trans. and ed. by Sears Jayne in *Marsilio Ficino's Commentary on Plato's Symposium* (Univ. of Missouri Studies, Vol. XIX, no. 1; Columbia, 1944), pp. 133–40.

21. See, e.g., *Theologica Platonica* XI.3, and the *Comment. in Plotin. Ennead.* I.6; *Opera Omnia*, pp. 241, 1574 ff.

22. The Latin, *a sensibus oritur*, contains this ambiguity: thought may originate in the senses, as Aristotle and Aquinas held, but it fulfills itself only in rising above the senses, as Plato held. See P.O. Kristeller, *The Philosophy of Marsilio Ficino*, trans. by Virginia Conant (New York, 1943), pp. 234 ff.

23. *De Amore* II.4, in Jayne, pp. 139–40.

24. *De Amore* II.6, in Jayne, pp. 140–41.

25. See vi.ix.20–23, the essence of which is in the final lines: "when I wearie am, I downe doe lay / My limbes in every shade, to rest from toyle." Melibee's counterpart in the pastoral spectrum of *As You Like It* (which dramatizes E.K.'s three modes) is Corin—see especially

III.ii.11–85. Melibee, whom commentators have atrociously glamorized, spouts a philosophy partly based on sour grapes: he worked for ten years as a gardener at court without getting ahead (ix.24–25). For all his self-sufficiency, Spenser kills him off in a hemistich (xi.18).

26. Lionel Trilling, "Dr. Leavis and the Moral Tradition," in *A Gathering of Fugitives* (Boston, 1956), p. 105.

27. Plato's *Ion* 533D is a familiar source for the figure of the poet as a bee in the muses' garden. This may also have suggested Spenser's Clarion, in *Muiopotmos,* whose behavior in his garden recalls that of the young poet, the first gift of delight in the nursery of commonplaces. Like the poet of Book VI, Clarion is ravished by the variety of the garden, but *his* meander is aimless and uncontrolled, a picking at choice bits.

28. In the *December* eclogue, Colin moves from literal rusticity back to the kind of metaphoric language with which he opened the *Calender,* thereby salvaging some symbolic possibilities from the wreckage left by the boors.

29. For the various problems connected with this allusion see the *Variorum* notes to IV.i.23 (Vol. IV, pp. 168–69) and VI.x.13 (Vol. VI, p. 251). If the battle of Centaurs and Lapiths was transferred from Pirithous' wedding in order to hint at a defect in Theseus and the consequent abandonment of Ariadne, this may point to the particular version of the myth Spenser had in mind: the one in which her pain was resolved in her second marriage to Bacchus, a love-death and apotheosis signified when the god enskied her crown. For the Neoplatonist motif, see Edgar Wind, *Pagan Mysteries in the Renaissance* (New Haven, 1958), pp. 130–31.

30. On the Graces, see Ernst Gombrich, "Botticelli's Mythologies: a Study in the Neoplatonic Symbolism of his Circle," *Journal of the Warburg and Courtauld Institutes,* VIII (1945), 32; André Chastel, *Marsile Ficin et L'art* (Geneva, 1954), pp. 146–47; D. T. Starnes, "Spenser and the Graces," *PQ,* XXI (July, 1942), 268–82; Wind, *Pagan Mysteries, passim.*

31. A passage by Wind describing the Neoplatonic dynamics of

symbolic thought is worth quoting because of its applicability to Spenser's method in this poem: "It follows that all mystical images, because they retain a certain articulation by which they are distinguished as 'hedges' or *umbraculae,* belong to an intermediate state, which involves further 'complication' above, and further 'explication' below. They are never final in the sense of a literal statement which would fix the mind to a given point; nor are they final in the sense of the mystical Absolute in which all images would vanish. Rather they keep the mind in continued suspense by presenting the paradox of an 'inherent transcendence'; they persistently hint at more than they say." *Pagan Mysteries,* p. 168.

SHERMAN HAWKINS

Mutabilitie and the Cycle of the Months

1. Quotations are from the Johns Hopkins Variorum Spenser and, unless otherwise noted, from the Mutabilitie Cantos. My obligations to Professors Bennett, Bush, Cumming, Stirling, and Tuve are obvious, as are my differences and agreements with other scholars. I am indebted to Dr. Richard Stockton's dissertation, "The Christian Content of Edmund Spenser's 'Mutabilitie' Cantos" (Princeton, 1954) for my interpretation of Nature, and to Dr. Thomas Roche for help in interpreting the Faunus episode and the mythological figures.

2. *The Allegory of Love* (Oxford, 1938), p. 354.

3. *Of the Lawes of Ecclesiasticall Politie* (London, 1594–97), p. 57. The argument of this paragraph is drawn largely from Hooker's first Book. For the figure of the circle, see Pierre de la Primaudaye, *The French Academie,* trans. by T.B.C. (London, 1618), p. 647.

4. Hooker, p. 81.

5. "An Hymne of Heauenly Beautie," ll. 200–201.

6. See Wisdom 7.29, 26: Wisdom is "more beautiful then the sunne," the "brightnes of the euerlasting light, the vndefiled mirroure of the maiestie of God." Biblical quotations follow the Geneva version of 1560 excepting the substitution of "unveiled" (Revised Standard

Version) for "open" in the epigraph, and "labour" (1611) for "studie" in Hebrews 9.11.

7. "An Hymne of Heauenly Beautie," l. 242.

8. *Two Bookes of Canstancie, Written in Latine by Iustus Lipsius,* trans. by Sir John Stradling ed. by Rudolf Kirk (New Brunswick, N.J., 1939), pp. 118, 106.

9. Lipsius, pp. 110–11, 102.

10. Hooker, p. 51.

11. "The Praise of Constancie," in *The Soule's Immortall Crowne* (1605) in *The Works in Verse and Prose of Nicholas Breton,* ed. by A. B. Grosart (2 vols.; Edinburgh, 1879), I, 20 B2ᵛ. Compare Spenser's Nature to Breton's Wisdom ("Vpon the Praise of Wisedom," *ibid.,* pp. 20 Bᵛ–20 B1).

12. Lewis, pp. 356–57.

13. Hence when Sir Henry Lee presented before her "An excellent Dialogue betweene Constancie and Inconstancie," the outcome was a foregone conclusion: Inconstancie finds herself drawn by the Queen's power "from the circle of my fancies, to the center of constant loue," and "changed to that estate which admitteth no change," to "be my selfe as she is, *Semper eadem." The Phoenix Nest, 1593,* ed. by Hyder E. Rollins (Cambridge, Mass., 1931), pp. 28–29. *The Phoenix Nest* assigns the last two phrases to *Const[ancie],* but two MSS give them to her opponent (pp. 137, 139, 141).

14. *The Third Part of the Countess of Pembrokes Yuychurch* (London, 1592), pp. 10ᵛ–11.

15. Fraunce, p. 43.

16. For Eden as a pastoral hill, comparable to other hills of legend, sacred and profane, see "Iulye" ll. 57 ff., and E.K.'s gloss. The parallelism between Arlo and Acidale is surely no accident: one is the favorite haunt of Diana, the other of Venus; Calidore, like Faunus, intrudes on naked goddesses; the Graces, like Diana, quit the mountain of their choice. The analogy suggests close connections between the Legends of Courtesy and Constancy: indeed, Calidore's abandonment of his quest raises the very problem to be resolved in the Cantos.

17. *Ovide moralisé en prose,* ed. by C. DeBoer, in *Verhandelingen der Koninklijke Nederlandse Akademie van Wetenschappen,* Vol. LXI, No. 2 (1954), p. 288.

18. Emile Mâle, *The Gothic Image,* trans. by Dora Nussey (New York, Harper Torchbooks, 1958), p. 66.

19. Pierre Bersuire, *Opera Omnia,* 6 vols. in 3 (Cologne, 1730), I, 247–48; II, 127–29; V, 42.

20. *Patrologia latina,* CXI, 302–3.

21. This paragraph is drawn from Sir W. W. Greg, "Old Style—New Style," in *Joseph Quincy Adams Memorial Studies,* ed. by James G. McManaway, *et al.* (Washington, 1948), pp. 563–69, and Reginald L. Poole, "The Beginning of the Year in the Middle Ages," *Proceedings of the British Academy,* X (1921–23), 113–37.

22. To distinguish the religious from the natural year as Spenser does in the *Calender* fits a more dualistic view of nature than I find in the Mutabilitie Cantos and helps explain the darker tone of the earlier poem. Cf. Robert Allen Durr, "Spenser's Calendar of Christian Time," *ELH,* XXIV (1957), 269–95.

23. *PL,* XXXVIII, 85. For a series of sixteenth-century paintings and engravings which merge the labors of the months with the parables of Christ, see Pierre Marie Auzas, "Les douze mois de Grimmer," *Pro Arte,* XVII (1948), 3–16.

24. In the satirical *Mother Hubberds Tale,* ll. 1–3, August is the month in which Astraea *leaves* the world. For full discussion of Astraea, see Frances A. Yates, "Queen Elizabeth as Astraea," *Journal of the Warburg and Courtauld Institutes,* X (1947), 27–82.

25. *De Consolatione Philosophiae,* IV, m. 6; III, m. 2, in *The Works of Geoffrey Chaucer,* ed. by F. N. Robinson, 2d ed. (Cambridge, Mass., 1957), pp. 371, 343.

26. The ages of the world were also analogous to the ages of man: see Rabanus Maurus, *PL,* CVII, 726–28, and Bede, *PL,* XC, 288. For an iconographical representation of the six ages of history as a circle, see British Museum Royal MS 19 C 1 f.58ᵛ.

27. The figure of the circle dominates the Cantos from the "euer-

whirling wheele / Of *Change"* in the first stanza to the great cycle of time in Canto 7: the changing significance of the figure reflects the development of the argument. Compare the emblem of a compass tracing a broken circle with the motto, "Labore et Constantia," in George Wither, *A Collection of Emblemes* (1635), reproduced in Rosemary Freeman, *English Emblem Books* (London, 1948), opposite p. 147. The emblem appears earlier on the title pages of Geoffrey Whitney, *A Choice of Emblemes* (London, 1586) and Alciati's *Emblemata* (Antwerp, 1581). Note the star-gazers in the background of Wither's version.

28. Compare the familiar political interpretation of the Phaeton story in which the "Bulls, Centaurs, Lyons, Scorpions, and such like" of the zodiac are interpreted as evil and seditious subjects (Fraunce, p. 35ᵛ). In an unusual fourteenth-century almanac (Vienna Nat. Bibl. Codex 1921), the signs of the zodiac attack or menace human figures— even the fish are shown biting a swimmer. But the zodiacal signs, like the months, were conventional figures capable of fresh interpretation: for examples of novel religious symbolism (Aries suggests the Paschal Lamb; Aquarius, the Baptist), see "The Columnes," ll. 520–549, in *Du Bartas His Second Weeke,* in *The Complete Works of Joshuah Sylvester,* ed. by A. B. Grosart (2 vols.; Edinburgh, 1880), I, 158–59.

29. Hooker, p. 54.

30. If a man loves righteousness, declares Solomon in the 1611 version, the labors of Wisdom are virtues: temperance and prudence, justice and fortitude (Wisdom 8.7).

31. Hebrews 4.9, 11.

32. I am assuming that this numbering is Spenser's, and that the Legend of Constancy follows that of Courtesy.

33. Spenser's sabbath, like the modern Sunday, combines the Jewish seventh day of rest with the Christian eighth (or first) day celebration of the resurrection of Christ. These correspond to the seventh age of the world, representing the repose of just souls, and the eighth age, representing their final resurrection (see Rabanus Maurus, *PL,* CVII, 726–28 and CXI, 299–300). For the symbolic values of seven

and eight, see Pietro Bongo, *Mysticae Numerorum Significationis Liber* (Bergamo, 1585). According to Hugh of St. Victor, numbers have significance by extension: thus seven beyond six represents rest after work, and eight beyond seven represents eternity after mutability. Vincent F. Hopper, *Medieval Number Symbolism* (New York, 1938), p. 101.

34. "An Hymne of Heauenly Beautie," ll. 295, 298–299.

35. Compare the beginning of Canto 7, where the poet's awe at the "too high flight" which he must undertake serves to emphasize the hardihood of Mutabilitie, the vain curiosity of Faunus. These utterances of the poet help direct the reader's attitude. We too are permitted to enter the councils of the gods, but Spenser warns us that the secrets of Providence are to be approached in the humility that waits upon divine illumination, not in the spirit of a prying astrologer or a rebellious titan. See Lipsius, p. 104: "The Auncientes haue fayned that Gyantes aduanced themselues against God, to pull him out of his throne. Let vs omitte these fables: In very trueth you querulous and murmuring men be these Gyantes." Compare Boethius, III, pr. 12, pp. 356–57.

36. Wisdom 7.17–19.

37. "*Iupiter* is commonly pictured sitting, sith the eternall Monarch of heauen, and earth, is alwaies immutable, one, and the same, and neuer subiect to any alteration" (Fraunce, p. 13). See also Vincenzo Cartari, *The Fountaine of Ancient Fiction,* trans. by Richard Linche (London, 1599), p. K2.

A. KENT HIEATT
The Daughters of Horus

1. A. Kent Hieatt, *Short Time's Endless Monument: the Symbolism of the Numbers in Edmund Spenser's Epithalamion* (New York, 1960).

2. Hieatt, pp. 16–30, 83–109.

3. The shrewdest test involves as little disturbance of my original

ordering of the stanzas as is compatible with changing it at all, for reasons which will be obvious to readers of my book. I suggest, for test purposes, the order 1–12, sequentially, against 14, 13, 16, 15, 18, 17, 20, 19, 22, 21, 24, 23. I have tried this ordering and found it hopeless, but my *parti pris* inevitably renders my results suspect.

4. All quotations follow the text of the Variorum Spenser, except that *i, u,* and *v* are normalized.

5. Hieatt, pp. 19, 20, 86, 87.

6. Hieatt, pp. 20, 21, 90, 91.

HALLETT SMITH
The Use of Conventions in Spenser's Minor Poems

1. *Elizabethan Poetry: A Study in Conventions, Meaning and Expression* (Cambridge, Mass., 1952).

2. *Works of Samuel Johnson,* VIII (New York, 1903), 85.

3. *The World's Body* (New York, 1938), pp. 1–28.

4. *American Journal of Philology,* XXXII (1911), 294–312.

5. *The Age of Chaucer,* ed. by Boris Ford (Penguin, 1954), p. 221.

6. *Minor Poems,* II, 599–608. Quotations are from the Variorum Edition, in which the *Minor Poems,* Vol. I (Baltimore, 1943) and Vol. II (Baltimore, 1947), comprise respectively Volumes VII and VIII.

7. D. C. Allen, *Image and Meaning* (Baltimore, 1960), pp. 20–41.

8. *Minor Poems,* II, 403.

9. *Minor Poems,* II, 603.

10. *Classical Mythology in Spenser's Poetry* (Princeton, 1932), p. 12.

11. *PMLA,* XLIII (1928), 646–74.

12. *Minor Poems,* I, 429.

13. *English Literature in the Sixteenth Century Excluding Drama* (Oxford, 1954), p. 370.

14. *The Poems of Sir Arthur Gorges,* ed. by Helen E. Sandison (Oxford, 1953), p. 237.

15. "Spenser and the Epithalamic Convention," *Comparative Literature,* IX (1957), 215–28.

16. *English Epithalamies,* ed. by R. H. Case (London, n.d.), pp. 1–3.

17. *Ibid.,* pp. 4–5.

18. Israel Baroway, "The Imagery of Spenser and the *Song of Songs,*" *JEGP,* XXXIII (1934), 23–45.

19. "The Tradition of Prothalamia," in *English Studies in Honor of James Southall Wilson* (Charlottesville, Va., 1951), pp. 223–41.

20. "Spenser's English Rivers," *Transactions of the Connecticut Academy of Arts and Sciences,* XXIII (1920), 65–108.

LOUIS L. MARTZ
The *Amoretti*

1. *The Elizabethan Love Sonnet* (London: Methuen, 1956), pp. 97–102.

2. See Janet Spens, *Spenser's Faerie Queene* (London: Arnold, 1934), p. 104.

3. See Hallett Smith, *Elizabethan Poetry* (Cambridge: Harvard Univ. Press, 1952), pp. 166–67.

4. This translation was suggested by my friend Thomas Bergin.

5. See *OED,* "By": A. *prep.,* IV, 26; and George Gascoigne, *A Hundreth Sundrie Flowres,* ed. by C. T. Prouty (Columbia: Univ. of Missouri, 1942), poems 10, 12, 14, pp. 114–16.

6. "The Imagery of Spenser and the *Song of Songs,*" *JEGP,* XXXIII (1934), 23–45; esp. pp. 39–40.

Supervising Committee, The English Institute, 1960

The Program

September 6 through September 9, 1960

I. Spenser's Minor Poems
   Directed by WILLIAM NELSON, *Columbia University*

1. Spenser's Use of Conventions in the Minor Poems
   HALLETT SMITH, *California Institute of Technology*

2. *The Amoretti*
   LOUIS L. MARTZ, *Yale University*

3. The Daughters of Horus: Order in the Stanzas of the *Epithalamion*
   A. KENT HIEATT, *Columbia University*

4. *Mutabilitie* and the Cycle of the Months
   SHERMAN HAWKINS, *Princeton University*

II. Whitman's OUT OF THE CRADLE ENDLESSLY ROCKING
   Directed by R. W. B. LEWIS, *Yale University*

1. "Out of the Cradle" in Context
   STEPHEN E. WHICHER, *Cornell University*

2. Whitman's Curious Warble: Reminiscence and Reconciliation
   PAUL FUSSELL, JR., *Rutgers University*

3. "Out of the Cradle" as a Romance
   RICHARD CHASE, *Columbia University*

4. Whitman Justified
ROY HARVEY PEARCE, *Ohio State University*

III. Problems of Textual Editing
Directed by VINTON DEARING, *University of California at Los Angeles*

1. Textual Problems in St. Thomas More's *Richard III*
RICHARD S. SYLVESTER, *Yale University*

2. Internal Evidence and the Attribution of Elizabethan Plays
SAMUEL SCHOENBAUM, *Northwestern University*

3. Problems in the Making of Computer Concordances
STEPHEN M. PARRISH, *Cornell University*

IV. A Critique of Myth Criticism
Directed by BERNARD SCHILLING, *University of Rochester*

1. Myth-making in Collins' "Ode on the Poetical Character" and Keats' "To Psyche"
HAROLD BLOOM, *Yale University*

2. Symbol and Idea in Collins' "Ode on the Poetical Character" and Keats' "To Psyche"
HOYT TROWBRIDGE, *University of New Mexico*

3. Dryden and the Conservative Myth: A Reading of "Absalom and Achitophel"
BERNARD SCHILLING, *University of Rochester*

Registrants, 1960

Meyer Howard Abrams, Cornell University; Ruth M. Adams, Douglass College; Paul J. Aldus, Ripon College; Gellert Spencer Alleman, Newark College of Arts and Sciences, Rutgers University; Paul J. Alpers, Harvard University; Reta Margaret Anderson, Woman's College, University of North Carolina; Robert W. Ayers, Georgetown University; Sheridan Baker, University of Michigan; C. Lombardi Barber, Amherst College; Isabel Harriss Barr (Mrs. Pietro Aria), Fordham University; Phyllis Bartlett, Queens College; F. W. Bateson, Oxford University; D. W. Becker, Miami University; Josephine Waters Bennett, Hunter College; Paul L. Bennett, Denison University; J. B. Bessinger, University College, Toronto; T. Whitney Blake; Harold Bloom, Yale University; Max Bluestone, Babson Institute; Muriel Bowden, Hunter College; Brother C. Francis Bowers, F.S.C., Manhattan College; Leicester Bradner, Brown University; Helene Maxwell Brewer, Queens College; Mary Campbell Brill, West Virginia Wesleyan College; Margaret M. Bryant, Brooklyn College; Mrs. W. Bryher; Jean R. Buchert, Woman's College, University of North Carolina; Brother Fidelian Burke, F.S.C., LaSalle College; Sister M. Vincentia Burns, O.P., Albertus Magnus College; Katherine Burton, Wheaton College; May D. Bush, Woman's College, University of North Carolina.

Grace J. Calder, Hunter College; Edward F. Callahan, College of the Holy Cross; Kenneth Neill Cameron; Norman Carlson, De Pauw University; Hugh C. G. Chase; Richard Chase, Columbia University;

James L. Clifford, Columbia University; Alice P. Comparetti, Colby College; Francis X. Connolly, Fordham University; Lester Conner, Columbia University; John S. Coolidge, Swarthmore College; T. W. Copeland, University of Massachusetts; Joan Elizabeth Corbett, Texas Woman's University; G. Armour Craig, Amherst College; Martha Alden Craig, Wellesley College; Lucille Crighton, Gulf Park College; James H. Croushore, Mary Washington College; Charles R. Crowe, University of Pittsburgh; J. V. Cunningham, Brandeis University; Curtis Dahl, Wheaton College; Charles T. Davis, Princeton University; Winifred M. Davis; Vinton Dearing, University of California, Los Angeles; Stuart H. L. Degginger, Hollins College; Robert M. Dell, Pace College; Charlotte D'Evelyn, Mount Holyoke College; E. T. Donaldson, Yale University; Sister Rose Barnard Donna, c.s.j., College of Saint Rose; Mother Mary of the Incarnation Dowd, o.s.u., College of New Rochelle; Edward R. Easton, Pace College; Ursula E. Eder, Brooklyn College; Martha England, Queens College; David V. Erdman, New York Public Library; Robert O. Evans, University of Kentucky; Alice M. Farrison, North Carolina College at Durham; W. Edward Farrison, North Carolina College at Durham; Edward G. Fletcher, University of Texas; Ephim G. Fogel, Cornell University; George H. Ford, University of Rochester; Frances A. Foster, Vassar College; Joseph Frank, University of Rochester; Robert W. Frank, Jr., Pennsylvania State University; Northrop Frye, Victoria College, University of Toronto; Edwin E. Fussell, Claremont Graduate School; Paul Fussell, Jr., Rutgers University.

Edward L. Galligan, Western Michigan University; Harold Garriott, De Pauw University; Sister Mary Cyrille Gill, Rosary College; Florence Gerdes, Ohio Northern University; Leonard Goldstein; Anthony Gosse, Bucknell University; T. J. Grace, s.j., Holy Cross College; John E. Grant, University of Connecticut; James Gray, Bishop's University; Richard Leighton Greene, Wesleyan University; Robert Halsband, Columbia University; John A. Hart, Carnegie University of Technology; Allen T. Hazen, Columbia University; Sherman Hawkins, Princeton University; Thelma J. Henner, Queens College; Ann

Louise Hentz, Lake Forest College; A. Kent Hieatt, Columbia University; Conrad Hilberry, De Pauw University; the Reverend William B. Hill, s.j., Novitiate of Saint Isaac Jogues; F. W. Hilles, Yale University; Stanley M. Holberg, St. Lawrence University; Norman N. Holland, Massachusetts Institute of Technology; J. L. Hollander, Yale University; Vivian C. Hopkins, College of Education, Albany; Lillian Herlands Hornstein, New York University; Muriel J. Hughes, University of Vermont; Julia Hysham, Skidmore College; Sister Mary Immaculate, o.p.; Ruth M. Jackson, Simpson College; George W. Johnson, Temple University; S. F. Johnson, Columbia University; Sister Julie, Rosary College; R. J. Kaufman, University of Rochester; Norman Kelvin, City College of New York; Karl Kiralis, St. Lawrence University; Clara M. Kirk, Douglass College; Herbert L. Kleinfield, Temple University; Carl F. Klinck, University of Western Ontario; Mary E. Knapp, Western College for Women; Kathrine Koller, University of Rochester; Karl Kroeber, University of Wisconsin; Frank A. Krutzke, Colorado College.

Craig La Drière, Catholic University of America; the Reverend John P. Lahey, s.j., Le Moyne College; Seymour Lainoff, Yeshiva College; Cecil Lang, Syracuse University; the Reverend Henry St. C. Levin, s.j., Loyola College; Lewis Leary, Columbia University; Dearing Lewis, Rockford College; Leon E. Lewis, Holy Cross College; R. W. B. Lewis, Yale University; Aharon Lichtenstein, Stern College of Yeshiva University; George de F. Lord, Yale University; Joseph P. Lovering, Canisius College; William F. Luebke, University of Denver; Charles J. McCann, Canisius College; John McChesney, Hotchkiss School; Jean MacIntyre, Kent State University; Richard A. Macksey, Johns Hopkins University; Kenneth MacLean, Victoria College, University of Toronto; Mother C. E. Maguire, Newton College of the Sacred Heart; Mother Saint Rita Marie, c.n.d., Notre Dame College of Staten Island; Kenneth B. Marshall, Denison University; Mary H. Marshall, Syracuse University; Thomas F. Marshall, Kent State University; Harold C. Martin, Harvard University; Louis L. Martz, Yale University; Donald C. Mell, Jr., University of Pennsylvania; Harrison

T. Mesrole, Pennsylvania State University; John H. Middendorf, Columbia University; Francis E. Mineka, Cornell University; Ruth Mohl, Brooklyn College; Mother Grace Monahan, o.s.u., College of New Rochelle; Ray Morrison, Los Angeles Valley College; William Nelson, Columbia University; the Reverend William T. Noon, s.j., Fordham University.

R. M. O'Clair, Harvard University; Mother E. O'Gorman, Manhattanville College of the Sacred Heart; the Reverend Joseph E. O'Neill, s.j., Fordham University; Ants Oras, University of Florida; Mother Thomas Aquinas O'Reilly, o.s.u., College of New Rochelle; James M. Osborn, Yale University; Stephen C. Paine, Salem College; Stephen M. Parrish, Cornell University; Edward B. Partridge, Bucknell University; Robert O. Payne, University of Cincinnati; Roy Harvey Pearce, Ohio State University; Norman Holmes Pearson, Yale University; Harry William Pedicord; Rainer Pineas, Pace College; Abbie F. Potts, Rockford College; Hereward T. Price, University of Michigan; George Foster Provost, Duquesne University; Max Putzel, University of Connecticut; the Reverend Charles J. Quirk, s.j., Loyola University; Warren Ramsey, University of California, Berkeley; Isabel E. Rathborne, Hunter College; Charles A. Ray, North Carolina College; Warner G. Rice, University of Michigan; David Allan Robertson, Jr., Barnard College; Thomas Roche, Princeton University; Leo Rockas, Wayne State University.

Henry W. Sams, Pennsylvania State University; Helen E. Sandison, Vassar College; Howard H. Schless, Columbia University; Helene B. M. Schnabel; Robert E. Scholes, University of Virginia; Flora Rheta Schreiber, New School for Social Research; Helen M. Scurr, University of Bridgeport; John T. Shawcross, Newark College of Engineering; Arthur Sherbo, Michigan State University; Agnes Sibley, Lindenwood College; Hallett Smith, California Institute of Technology; the Reverend Paul F. Smith, s.j., Creighton University; J. Gordon Spaulding, University of British Columbia; Robert D. Spector, Long Island University; Barbara Swain, Vassar College; Richard S. Sylvester, Yale University; Ruth Zabriskie Temple, Brooklyn College; Jonathan Thomas,

Rutgers University; Doris S. Thompson, Russell Sage College; William B. Todd, University of Texas; A. R. Towers, Queens College; Hoyt Trowbridge, University of New Mexico; Sister Rose Cecilia Varley, c.s.j., College of Saint Rose; Howard P. Vincent, Illinois Institute of Technology; the Reverend Vianney Vornwald, o.f.m., Siena College; Eugene M. Waith, Yale University; Andrew J. Walker, Georgia Institute of Technology; Howard J. Waskow, Yale University; Charlotte Crawford Watkins, Howard University; Minnie Wells, University of Alaska; Philip Wheelwright, University of California at Riverside; Mother Elizabeth S. White, Newton College of the Sacred Heart; Brother Joseph Wiesenfarth, f.s.c., De La Salle College; Edward K. Williams, De Pauw University; W. K. Wimsatt, Jr., Yale University; Samuel K. Workman, Illinois Institute of Technology; Philip Young, Pennsylvania State University; J. Zeldin, Hollins College.